WEIGHTLESS

Weightless

Making
Peace
With
Your
Body

KATE WICKER

SERVANT
BOOKS

PUBLISHED BY ST. ANTHONY MESSENGER PRESS
CINCINNATI, OHIO

Unless otherwise noted, Scripture passages have been taken from the *Revised Standard Version*, Catholic edition. Copyright ©1946, 1952, 1971 by the Division of Christian Education of the National Council of Churches of Christ in the USA. Used by permission. All rights reserved.

Scripture passages marked *NRSV* have been taken from *New Revised Standard Version Bible*, copyright ©1989 by the Division of Christian Education of the National Council of the Churches of Christ in the U.S.A., and used by permission. All rights reserved.

Quotes are taken from the English translation of the *Catechism of the Catholic Church* for the United States of America (indicated as *CCC*), 2nd ed. Copyright 1997 by United States Catholic Conference—Libreria Editrice Vaticana.

Cover design by Connie Gabbert
Cover image © iStockphoto | Okea
Book design by Mark Sullivan

LIBRARY OF CONGRESS CATALOGING-IN-PUBLICATION DATA
Wicker, Kate.
Weightless : making peace with your body / Kate Wicker.
p. cm.
Includes bibliographical references.
ISBN 978-0-86716-971-3 (alk. paper)
1. Catholic women—Religious life. 2. Body image in women—Religious aspects—Catholic Church. 3. Self-acceptance in women—Religious aspects—Catholic Church. I. Title.
BX2353.W53 2011
248.8'43—dc23
2011014535

ISBN 978-0-86716-971-3

Copyright ©2011, Kate Wicker. All rights reserved.

Published by Servant Books,
an imprint of St. Anthony Messenger Press
28 W. Liberty St.
Cincinnati, OH 45202
www.AmericanCatholic.org
www.ServantBooks.org

Printed in the United States of America.
Printed on acid-free paper.
11 12 13 14 15   5 4 3 2 1

dedication

To Dave, my best friend,
who always makes me feel beautiful
and loves me unconditionally.
I can't wait to grow old with you
—wrinkles and all!

And to my daughters:
You are lovely in every way.

c o n t e n t s

f o r e w o r d

When I was seventeen years old, I came across a chart in a magazine that listed height and weight figures that were in the range of anorexia. I found my height on the chart, then traced my finger down to look for my weight (which I knew well since I had weighed myself for the third time that morning just a few moments before). I found the square on the chart that represented the intersection, and it was colored red. There it was, clear as day. My height and weight were within the range of clinical anorexia.

I spent a long time staring at the data, rolling it over in my mind. And then I thought: How weird that someone so fat could make it on this chart!

I grew up in a culture where women had been taught that to be pretty is to have value—and it wasn't our grandmothers' definition of "pretty," where sparkling eyes or a gracious smile were valued along with other parts of a woman's physical appearance. This new view of how women should look was driven by a lust-saturated culture, where a woman could hardly consider herself attractive if she didn't have the physique of a Vegas showgirl. Fashion trends pushed revealing outfits that were unforgiving of the slightest imperfections, and popular media reinforced the subtle message that being a complete, fulfilled woman wasn't possible without having the body mass index of an Olympic athlete and the abdomen of a thirteen-year-old boy. I once noticed at a grocery store checkout line that every single one of the magazines in front of me made the promise that it would teach its readers how to be "sexy." I received the message loud and clear: You are only as valuable as you are attractive.

And the pressure didn't stop there. This warped view of the way a woman should look was only one part of a larger unbalanced world-view. The culture that surrounded us had lost the concept that each one of us is a cherished child of God, and we tried to fill the vacuum that resulted by seeking value and acceptance somewhere else. We defined ourselves by our careers, our material possessions, our diets, or whatever the latest worldly measure of a person's worth was. And, of course, for women especially, the pressure to define ourselves by our physical appearance was always there.

This is how I could stare in a mirror when I was seventeen and see nothing but imperfections. Not only was I comparing myself to unrealistic images in the media, but I had no clue where my value as a person really lay. I didn't understand that as long as I looked to a number on the scale or a checklist on a diet plan or some other worldly measure for a sense of fulfillment, I was doomed to a life of restless searching, always feeling imperfect and incomplete.

It wasn't until I converted to Catholicism when I was in my late twenties that I finally made peace with my body, and with my whole self as a woman. The ancient wisdom of the Church taught me what it means to be truly feminine—and it didn't require being able to fit into a certain dress size. It taught me the difference between respecting my body as a temple of the Holy Spirit and obsessing over its imperfections to try to fit in with the world. And, most importantly, it taught me that my value as a human being and a woman comes from God.

It took me years to even be able to grasp the Church's body of thought on on all these matters. Catholic wisdom on personhood and femininity is like a treasure chest the size of a lake, and I'm sure countless other women have felt excited but overwhelmed at the prospect of sifting through it all. Finally, thanks to Kate Wicker, we have it all distilled into one very readable, deeply personal book.

Weaving powerful stories from her own life with wisdom from Scripture, Church documents, and the lives of the saints, Kate walks us through her own transformation from a scared young girl at war with her body to a Catholic woman who has found peace and healing in the Lord. Any woman who has ever felt driven to find meaning and acceptance in her external appearance will see something familiar in every chapter and will find words of comfort and solace on every page. Through hard data and real-life anecdotes, Kate reminds us that the values of the world place burdens on our shoulders that can drag us down, sometimes to the point of being crushed, but if we allow ourselves to be carried along by God's love, we will find that we become weightless.

—Jennifer Fulwiler

acknowledgments

Writing a book is never a solo project. I am grateful to many individuals who helped this book come to fruition. To name only a few: Cindy Cavanar for believing in me and the story I felt called to tell. Cathy Adamkiewicz, if not for your generosity, support, and humility, this book would have never been coaxed into existence. These pages are yours as much as they are mine. To Lucy Scholand, my patient editor, you helped me to find the right words (and cut some of the unnecessary ones) when I failed to do so on my own. I thank my blog readers for blessing me with their emails, comments, and encouragement, and for helping me to see that I might have something worthwhile to share. Mom and Dad, thank you for your constant support. You always said I'd write a book someday. Well, now I have. Pop, your free, dependable, and quality babysitting services during the early writing process were invaluable. To my children, you are and always will be my most important works in progress. Dave, you're more than a husband. You're a real helpmate. Thanks for being my go-to guy. And last but never least, thank you to my Heavenly Father for gifting me with the right words. Anything in these pages that does not heal ended up here only because I wasn't listening well enough to You.

introduction

I was nine years old when it first struck me that I was fat. I was in a doctor's office, and the stiff, crinkly paper sheet that covered the examination table was sticking to the back of my thighs. My arms were as bruised as ripe bananas. So was my fragile ego.

A nurse had spent several minutes repeatedly poking my skin, unsuccessfully trying to find a vein for a routine blood draw. She finally shook her head and admitted defeat. "I'm so sorry. I just can't get a vein."

The obvious explanation—obvious to me anyway—was that this was somehow my fault, my body's fault. There was too much skin and fat to get through to find a vein. I blinked back the tears. My mom and the nurse assumed I was crying from the physical pain, but that wasn't it at all. I was convinced that the beautiful me was hidden inside dense layers of fat.

A doctor finally found a vein. He gently patted my arm—"You trouper, you"—and apologized. He said something about my veins being thin. *At least something about me is thin,* I thought. He did not mention my thick, impervious skin. But I was convinced that I was to blame for eating too many Little Debbies after school.

After my doctor's appointment my mom bought me a Snow White poster as a reward for my courage. But instead of lifting my spirits, seeing the princess chipped away at my eggshell ego. Every time I caught a glance of that porcelain-skinned beauty, I was reminded that she was everything I was not. Snow White was thin. She was beautiful. And all her admiring dwarves knew it.

Aiming for Perfection

My parents never put much emphasis on looks. I was the only daughter in my family, and they filled me with as much love as they possibly could. Somehow they didn't see my desperate longing to be beautiful. They didn't know the depths of my hurt until many years later, when I was diagnosed with a clinical eating disorder.

I've often tried to figure out where my self-loathing stemmed from and why I was so desperate for the approval of others. My mom was never overly vain, and my eating disorder confounded her, since she'd never had an issue with food or her body. But she was beautiful (inside and out), and I do remember wishing I could be more like her. Everyone always commented on how pretty she was. When people saw me, with my round face and my smile obscured by orthodontia, they'd say things like, "Oh, you must look like your dad."

Despite feeling uncomfortable in my own skin and enduring "Miss Piggy" name calling, I was always aware of my parents' and God's love for me—even when others shunned me. I remember deciding when I was eleven or so, after I'd been teased by some boys for being chubby, that if I couldn't be the pretty or thin girl, then I'd work on being the responsible, obedient, smart, and even funny one. Then, I hoped, people might learn to like me.

I was the second child in my family, and my older brother grappled with a drug addiction during my childhood. Since my parents were constantly trying to fix him, I decided to fine-tune myself so well, so perfectly, that they wouldn't ever have to worry about fixing me. My aim was to please. Not surprisingly, I became a rigid perfectionist.

I poured myself into academics, always wanting to earn top marks and to make my friends and family happy and proud of me. My favorite activity was horseback riding. I found comfort on those big animals, where I felt small, something I longed to be.

I had no trouble making new friends. Boys never noticed me, or if they did, it was because I made them laugh, not swoon. But that was OK. Eventually I started finding self-acceptance. It didn't matter that I wasn't as stick-thin as my friends. I didn't wince too much when the mother of one of them pulled my hand away from a plate of treats and then questioned whether I should be nibbling on a cookie. I cried only a little when some boys oinked at me as I walked to the school bus. I believed my parents and my horseback riding instructor when they said I was strong and athletic.

"It's what's on the inside that counts," my mom constantly reminded me. And I almost believed her—until something surprising happened: People started telling me I was pretty.

Extreme Makeover

The summer before my sophomore year in high school, I blossomed. My mom had always said she'd been a late bloomer, and I guess I was too. I transformed from a brace-faced, awkward, and pudgy little girl into a curvy young woman. I'll never forget the first day of school that year. Some of my peers didn't even recognize me. A lot of girls asked me in hushed voices what my "secret" was. I had no secret other than late puberty.

Boys started to notice, too. Those who had never approached me in anything other than a platonic or teasing way now flirted with me. It was exciting and scary at the same time. When I won a student council race and snagged a date to a school dance, I realized I was no longer a complete nerd.

Every girl's dream, right?

For someone already prone to perfectionism and people pleasing, it quickly became a nightmare. My newfound popularity and attention delivered a very clear message: I was easier to like being pretty; I was closer to my ideal being thin. This knowledge piled pressure on me—pressure to be thin, to be beautiful, to be smart but not too smart. Even though I was the same girl on the inside—a goofy drama queen who loved horses, singing, and reading—how I looked on the outside suddenly made me more important.

Was I happier now that I was the girl I'd always hoped to be? Far from it. Instead, I became a vain and obsessive swan who lived in constant fear that if I wasn't careful, I'd morph back into my old, ugly duckling self. And this marked the beginning of a long, tortuous relationship with food and weight.

There came a point at which no one complimented me anymore. It felt as if everyone had stopped noticing me. So I decided I needed to get thinner. I started dieting and running, too. I'd run at least six miles every day, rain or shine. I couldn't control who accepted me and who didn't, but I could control how much I weighed.

One day I was sitting with a big group of my girlfriends at a restaurant. They were all eating typical teenage fare—greasy burgers, French fries, and milkshakes. I picked at a salad without any dressing on it.

"Aren't you hungry?" a friend asked.

Yes, I'm starving for control and love and acceptance. That's what my sickness was saying. But I lied and told her I'd already eaten.

At first I felt jealous of my friends for the way they could sip milkshakes without considering their calorie count, but then I started to feel powerful, superior. "I can resist eating. I can get thinner. I'm stronger than they are."

It didn't take long for the curves I'd formed to vanish. Zero became my holy grail of clothing sizes. Ironic that the number means an absence of anything, because that is exactly what I was trying to fill—the nothingness in my heart.

My parents started to get worried. "You're too thin, Katie. Please eat," my mom begged.

Always a people-pleaser, I answered my mother's plea. I started eating again. Food tasted so good. But when I saw that little red line climbing on the scale, I panicked. I felt out of control.

When I lost weight, the scale was my cheerleader, applauding me for being "strong." Now suddenly it reared its ugly head and screamed at me, berating me for letting myself go. The barometer of my self-worth betrayed me.

Then I read about a girl who suffered from bulimia. How easy it was to purge herself of the demons that haunted her—extra calories and fat. She would gorge on cream-filled donuts and plate-sized cookies, only to regurgitate the food and watch it disappear down the toilet. This unknown woman became my mentor.

I was never gluttonous—no eating frenzies for me. I simply used bulimia as a way to hide my eating disorder. My parents wanted me to eat, so I did. But I couldn't stand the feeling of food swimming in my stomach. I had to get it out. I had to purge myself of my weakness. No matter the cost, I had to stay thin.

Hitting Rock Bottom

I spent most of my adolescence at war with my body. I'd experience brief periods of healthfulness, but it never lasted. Like most addicts—and I was addicted to the pursuit of thinness—I had to hit rock bottom before I could be saved. My rock bottom happened in college.

A brief stint with a nutrition counselor during my senior year of high school had helped me to adopt more healthful habits and maintain a healthy weight, but my body image was still shaky. Most of the time I didn't see myself as thin enough or good enough. When I was twenty-one a bad breakup resurrected my old inner demons. As I tried to piece my broken heart back together, I'd often find myself weeping and reeling for control. Here I was at the cusp of college graduation, feeling utterly alone and not sure what I was going to do with my life. Everything around me was unraveling.

But I knew how to knit it back together. There was a way to make myself feel more powerful and get a grasp on all the loose strings of my life. I drastically cut my calorie intake. I went to the gym twice a day. I purged myself of the food I did eat by throwing up or taking laxatives. All those healthy habits I'd worked so hard to bring back into my life took a backseat to my pursuit of thinness.

My restrictive diet and purging left me feeling high at first. Then I'd feel the emptiness. My stomach was hungry, and so was my soul.

I was constantly sick, and I was always cold. My menstrual cycle went away, which scared me, because I had started thinking about my fertility and what a gift it was. I was terrified that I wouldn't be able to have children. Not surprisingly, I cried a lot. I prayed too, because I knew that what I really needed was the awareness of God's mercy and love for me.

After a church retreat I decided I was tired of being at war with my body. I told my parents I needed help. I was fortunate, because insurance covered my therapy. I was diagnosed with a clinical eating disorder.

I began therapy that lasted almost two years and carried me through my senior year of college as well as my first year in the real world. I slowly reshaped the image I had of myself. I stopped stepping on the scale ten times a day. I was reunited with an old friend from high school, and we began dating. I was upfront with him about my body-image struggles, my eating disorder, and the fact that I was in therapy. He accepted this. He accepted me. He would later become my husband and the first man I was romantically involved with who would and still does love me unconditionally.

From the outside I looked completely whole and healthy. I was no longer purging. I was running for the health of it, not as a punitive measure. I listened to my body and tried to eat when I was hungry and stop when I was satisfied. But even when my clinical eating disorder was reined in, the scale—instead of my God—was too often my go-to gauge for my self-worth. I realized that, while I'd put an end to my self-destructive behaviors and was physically "recovered," I was still spiritually sick.

So instead of turning solely to counselors, friends, or family for help, I looked to my God for inner healing. And that's when I really started to feel beautiful. This beauty had absolutely nothing to do with the number on the scale or the reflection in the mirror.

Women at War With Their Bodies

In the United States, as many as ten million women and a million men have clinical eating disorders, according to the National Eating Disorders Association.[1] (Although this book focuses on women's body-image problems, an increasing number of men are dissatisfied with their bodies and are spending inordinate amounts of money and time to improve their looks.)

Statistics like this don't begin to address the wave of body dissatisfaction sweeping across society. Whenever I write or speak about my body angst, countless women confide in me that they often don't feel thin, pretty, young, or good enough. The sad truth is, it would be difficult to find a woman who has not struggled with the way she looks, her relationship with food, or how much she weighs at some point in her life.

There are women who agonize over the size of their thighs; women who have jumped on the "no carb" bandwagon and banished bread—

even the whole-grain variety—from their diet in an effort to shed weight quickly; women who are slaves to the scale, the fridge, or the treadmill; women who are always on a diet yet remain overweight.

I've often wondered if we've forgotten how to eat. We eat either too little or too much. And even after we have cleaned our plates or banned entire food groups from our diets, we are still not happy or satisfied.

There are women with other body-image issues. Some think more about what they're going to wear than how to live a fuller, richer life. Others obsess about erasing wrinkles and augmenting breasts. Some anxiously look for that first gray hair.

It's no wonder, then, that bookstores' self-help sections are well-stocked with tomes on how to overcome body-image problems, how to love your body and make peace with it, and how to eat well and exercise without going to extreme measures. Yet you'd be hard-pressed to find a book that takes a faith-based, much less Catholic, approach to self-healing.

I know, because in my own struggles I bought dozens of books on the topic, and while some offered New-Agey mantras like "Let me be filled with light, not calories," none seemed to address the truth I needed to see: That reclaiming good health and a positive body image demands that you love yourself, and a healthy measure of self-love is very, very difficult when God is not at the center of your life. You can believe in God, but until you believe in his love for you, you cannot be freed of your obsession—whether it's with food, your looks, or your weight.

I love my Catholic faith, and it has played an immeasurable role in helping me make peace with my body. That's why I felt called to write this book. *Weightless* is not only for women like me who have faced an eating disorder but for any woman who is trying to spackle God-shaped holes with thinness, physical beauty, youth, or food. Each chapter includes a personal anecdote that marbles in tips I've found helpful to embrace in my own journey of healing; a "Soul Food" section that provides you with inspiring quotes, spiritual and practical tools, and tips to encourage, edify, and help you overcome your struggles; a meditation that offers imagery—something visual other than your own reflection—to focus on; and a prayer.

There are also discussion questions, "For Your Reflection," at the end of each chapter. These can be for your personal use or for use in a group.

It's my hope that this book and the tenets of our Christian faith might help reshape the way women look at themselves, others, and food and how we define what is beautiful. This book is not a substitute for therapy or treatment if you're dealing with an eating disorder, depression, anxiety, or some other mental health condition. Nor is it a diet book. It won't help you look like a supermodel. But I pray it might help you detach yourself from anything—food, the scale, flawless skin, dreams of curvier hips—that keeps you from growing closer to God.

"No eye has seen, nor ear heard, nor the heart of man conceived"— nor the scale or the mirror ever shown you—"what God has prepared for those who love him" (1 Corinthians 2:9). So let's start loving him by loving ourselves.

God bless.

chapter one

Media: The Distorted Mirror

When I was around twelve years old and becoming more aware of my clothing choices, I began to keep what I referred to as my "fashion inspiration notebook." As I came across styles of clothing or hairdos I liked in magazines or catalogues that came in the mail, I'd clip the pictures and tape them onto the pages of a spiral notebook. However, what was supposed to encourage creativity in my fashion choices soon became something that inspired inferiority and discontent. It made me aware of everything I wasn't and of all my body's imperfections.

There was one model in particular who was popular at the time who appeared frequently in the pages of my journal. She had long, blonde hair, and so did I, so I thought that maybe there was hope that I could also one day have her perfectly symmetrical face and athletic, thin figure. I'd stare at her images and feel envy or inadequacy. I wasn't even paying attention to her clothing anymore. I wanted her skin and her measurements.

Thankfully, I threw away that notebook when I grew older. But I couldn't shut out all of the images of beautiful women in the media that confronted me nearly every day. I still can't. I'm not twelve anymore, and I wouldn't dream of piecing together a collage of perfect beauties. Yet there are days when I'm still tempted to compare myself to these unrealistic ideals.

Maybe I'll watch a movie in which the female star flashes across the screen, fighting bad guys in her ultraskinny pants while maintaining perfectly coiffed hair. Or perhaps I'll pick up a gallon of milk when a smiling cutout model trying to sell me potato chips (as if she ever eats potato chips with a body like that) catches my eye. I have to stop myself and remember that these flawless images of women are not the norm.

A handful of the actresses and models that dominate advertisements, television, the catwalk, and the silver screen may be naturally blessed with their beauty and trim physiques. Many also have their images digitally altered before they appear, creating an even more unattainable "perfection." But a lot of these women pay a premium price to attain that kind of beauty. Some work out for hours a day and eat meals prepared by personal chefs. Others are always on severe diets. Some even go under the knife to achieve the kind of results they want.

It doesn't really matter how they've acquired their beauty—naturally or not. I should not compare myself to them. I should not be envious but appreciative of the gift of beauty they possess. I should remind myself that God is not a Hollywood producer or a fashion designer, and he creates people of all shapes and sizes. Some of us have great hair. Some of us have lovely, natural smiles. Some of us are naturally strong. Some of us have to work hard to get any muscle definition. But we are all worthy of his love.

Mirror, Mirror

If I sometimes find it hard to resist the siren song of beauty portrayed in the media, then is it any surprise that even the youngest children are already looking to the mirror for affirmation? "Mirror, Mirror, on the wall, who's the fairest of them all?" they ask, and they're not playing pretend. Our children are exposed to airbrushed and sexualized images of beautiful people everywhere—from billboards to magazines in the pediatrician's office. Then there are the ubiquitous, commercialized images of perfect, pretty princesses, who not only live happily ever after but always have good hair days and sparkling gowns to bedazzle onlookers.

It's not enough to pretend you're a princess in a far-off land. Marketers target the youngest of our children with princess packages. You want to be Cinderella? Then wear this silvery-blue gown (it only costs forty dollars!). And don't forget the glass slippers (they're half the price of the dress!).

"Diet Secrets of the Stars," "Lose Ten Pounds in a Week," "Miracle Wrinkle Cream Erases Crow's-Feet." The headlines rotate, but the theme remains the same: If you lose those last five, ten, fifteen, or twenty-plus pounds, embrace a starlet's measurements and beauty routine, and stop aging in its tracks, you'll be happier.

And so the brainwashing begins young. The mirror becomes distorted. By the time we reach adulthood and often much earlier, we no longer see our bodies for what they can do but only for how they look.

I'm not against girls playing princess; my daughters do it all of the time. Nor do I believe all media are evil. But we do have to be mindful of the messages that penetrate our own and our children's minds. Given my eating-disordered past, I've made an effort to be extra vigilant about the media my children consume, and my husband is with me on this. We've banned commercials from our home; my daughters watch either DVDs or public television. When we read fairy tales about princesses dressing in fancy gowns and going to the ball, we also stress that kindness is what makes people truly beautiful. But I've learned that even parents who are strict with their kids' media diet cannot completely shield them from the onslaught of messages that youth, beauty, and thinness are to be exalted and pursued with evangelical fervor. The society we live in makes it nearly impossible to keep children immune to the suggestion that a younger look and a slimmer silhouette comprise the pie in the sky.

Once I was plopping food down at the grocery checkout when I noticed one of my daughters, who was around four at the time, staring at a seductive chocolate cake on the cover of a popular women's magazine. Immediately next to the ooey-gooey deliciousness—dubbed "a slice of heaven"—was a popular movie star sporting a skimpy bikini.

"Doesn't that look good, Mommy?" my daughter said, thankfully pointing to the piece of cake and not the superslim movie star. And it did. But I couldn't help but wonder what kind of message that magazine rack was sending to our children and all of us. "Find your slice of heaven in a piece of cake! Then exercise obsessively to burn all that fat off, so you can look like this unhealthy and unrealistic representation of humanity."

Made in God's Image
The messages in the media are powerful to our children and to us. Yet God is bigger than any billboard showcasing a curvy, flawless woman. I know, because it was my faith in my Creator that eventually helped me see myself in a new, more forgiving light than that of *People* magazine.

When I was a young girl, I caved in to the societal pressure to be thin. I bought into the media's unrealistic ideal, stopped eating, and began seeing myself through a distorted mirror. It was like being trapped in a carnival fun house. Every mirror reflection I saw of myself was distorted.

Not everyone gobbles up the delicious eye candy in the media and allows the desire to emulate a celebrity push them over the edge.

Clinical eating disorders are complex psychological syndromes that transcend dieting or a yearning to look a certain way. But it's difficult not to get mixed up about what's important in life when everywhere you turn there's some new trendy diet or a picture of a perfect Hollywood beauty smiling at you with gleaming teeth.

Back in college I wrote a research paper on television's portrayal of females and how it affected college-aged women's body images. I conducted primary research as part of the paper, randomly selecting college women to complete a survey about their television viewing habits and their perceptions of the actresses on popular television shows at the time, such as *Friends*. I also included questions that analyzed how they felt about their bodies.

The results were shocking and oddly comforting to me at the same time, because they made me feel less alone in my body angst. Most respondents strongly agreed with the statement that television actresses were unrealistically thin. Yet a similarly high number strongly agreed that they often compared themselves to those actresses. What was really scary was that more than 30 percent of the respondents agreed that they would give up ten years of their life to be ten pounds thinner.

What's wrong with this picture? A whole lot, obviously.

It's tempting to place full blame on the media, and for a long time, I did just that: I blamed Hollywood for making me hate my body. Now, there's certainly a need to reassess how we look at the barrage of airbrushed, flawless, and ageless images that dominate television, the pages of magazines, billboards, advertisements, and the silver screen. But it's time we take some of the blame, too.

As I dealt with my eating disorder, I had to face the truth that there was something wrong with the picture in my head. And the media didn't draw this distorted picture; I did. I had forgotten a fundamental truth of our Christian faith: I am made in the image of God, not the media.

It seems many women have forgotten this truth. Whether we're bemoaning wrinkles, a few extra pounds, or the freckles on our faces, what we're really doing is questioning God's taste. God tells us everyone has value. So we can't buy into society's line of thinking—about ourselves or others. For today, fix your eyes on Christ, not on glossy magazines.

One way to stay more centered on Christ and to resist the temptation to compare your body to unrealistic images is to go on a media "fast." Perhaps you are careful about what media your children are exposed to, but what about you?

Whenever I'm feeling particularly vulnerable to body bashing, I cut unhealthy media from my life (think any fashion magazine you find at the checkout line of the grocery store) and instead focus on doing something healthy, like going on a walk or taking a time out with God. I've accepted that dealing with the temptation to chastise my body is my daily bread. Subsequently I have to make a conscious effort to open my eyes and see that my body—with all its real or alleged imperfections—is one of God's masterpieces.

Another way to come closer to body acceptance is to invite the mirror to be a loving advocate rather than a harsh critic. During my therapy, a counselor encouraged me to see my body as a whole, rather than breaking it down into separate flawed pieces ("I hate my stomach;" "My arms are too flabby;" "My eyes are squinty"). I was encouraged to stand in front of a mirror and take everything in, to see my body as a lovely ensemble. I encourage you to give it a try.

It may feel uncomfortable at first to look at your body in such an exposed manner, but it will get easier with time. Study your reflection, and when a disparaging thought pops into your head, counter it with a compliment. For instance, if you start to obsess over the size of your thighs, think about how strong your legs are, that they can carry you throughout your day.

Then think about what you love about your body—things that have nothing to do with your appearance. Maybe you have a lyrical voice. Perhaps your womb has carried children, or your legs have run a 5K. Focus on what you have accomplished with your body rather than the way it looks. Then take a deep breath, and step away from the mirror.

When I'm fighting the temptation to compare myself to Hollywood starlets, I like to look to the saints for inspiration. However, I've learned that artists have often idealized the physical appearances of saints. The Church's paintings, stained glass windows, and statues depict outward beauty as signs of these holy individuals' inner beauty and piety. Yet many probably fell way short of physical perfection. They were ordinary and even plain-looking people. Yet their souls were resplendent, and the glory of God shone in their lives and even in their faces.

My daughters frequently comment on pretty St. Cecilia and lovely Mary when we're looking through our saint books. I show them pictures of modern-day saints, too, of whom we have actual photos. Take Mother Teresa, for instance. Her diminutive stature and plain looks do not match society's standards of beauty. Yet her good deeds and her thirst for Christ made her resplendent and drew people to her. People saw goodness, love, and Jesus in her.

We're called to be saints, too. We probably won't manifest visible halos or porcelain skin, but we can bring others to Christ by leading holy lives.

When all else fails—when you find little inspiration in the saints, and you're not happy with what you see in the mirror—remember this: God not only loves you always but designed you, too. When I'm faced with an "ugly day" or am tempted to compare myself to a beautiful woman I encounter in the media or in real life, I remind myself that God "formed my inward parts, [he] knitted me together in my mother's womb" (Psalm 139:13). God knew me long ago, and he really does love me just the way I am.

"Wonderful are [his] works!" (Psalm 139:14). And I am, amazingly, one of his works. You are, too. That should be enough to give our body image a boost.

Soul Food

Make St. Thérèse of Lisieux your supermodel—your super role model, that is. The Little Flower of Jesus and Mary approached her faith, others, and herself with childlike confidence and humility. She performed no brilliant works before her death at the young age of twenty-four. Yet she abandoned herself to God and always thought of ways to deny herself to more perfectly follow Jesus.

In her autobiography, *The Story of a Soul*, St. Thérèse speaks of a certain nun who grated on her nerves. St. Thérèse hid her irritation and made every effort to be kind to the nun. She writes, "I was sure this would greatly delight Jesus, for every artist likes to have his works praised and the divine Artist of souls is pleased when we do not halt outside the exterior of the sanctuary where He has chosen to dwell but go inside to admire its beauty."

One day the nun asked, "Sister Thérèse, will you please tell me what attracts you so much to me? You give me such a charming smile whenever we meet." Thérèse knew: "Ah! It was Jesus hidden in the depth of her soul who attracted me, Jesus who makes the bittersweet things sweet!"[1]

Like St. Thérèse, let us see Jesus not only in everyone we encounter but in ourselves as well. Consider these words from the *Catechism of the Catholic Church*, "Being in the image of God the human individual possesses the dignity of a person, who is not just something, but someone" (*CCC*, #357).

Start seeing your body in a new light (nonfluorescent, of course). Whenever you're tempted to wish you were thinner, curvier, taller, shorter, or younger, remember that your body shares in the dignity of the image of God. You are a human being, not a human body.

Take to heart the Lord's advice to Samuel when he was directing him to the next king of Israel: "Do not look on his appearance or on the height of his stature...for the LORD sees not as man sees; man looks on the outward appearance, but the LORD looks on the heart" (1 Samuel 16:7). Don't make assumptions based on a person's external appearance. Look more deeply into others—and into yourself.

A journalist once asked Mother Teresa what it felt like to be referred to as a "living saint." She responded, "I'm very happy if you can see Jesus in me, because I can see Jesus in you. Holiness is not just for a few people. It's for everyone, including you, sir."[2]

We are not all called to have the measurements of a supermodel, but we are all called to strive for holiness. People discovered Jesus in Mother Teresa; let's pray they discover Jesus in us, too.

Meditation

Have you noticed how babies delight in their reflections? When they catch glimpses of themselves in a mirror, they smile, squeal, or laugh. When my girls were babies, they would even lean toward the mirror to give their images big wet kisses.

How many of us ever feel like kissing the reflection that stares back at us when we give ourselves the once-over in what might be more aptly referred to as the "lambasting glass" than the "looking glass"? The truth is, when faced with our images, many of us stop liking what we see. *That big pimple on my chin sure isn't pretty. My arms aren't toned enough. My backside looks bigger today than it did yesterday. Wouldn't it be nice to look more like so-and-so?*

You get the picture.

But God doesn't see that picture. He doesn't see what we see at all. God loves what he created—curvy, rifle-thin, disabled, or disfigured. We're his art, his creation.

When we criticize our reflections, we're not seeing clearly. We're blind to the kind of pure, unconditional love that God has for each of us.

For today, try to look at your reflection in the mirror through God's eyes. Look past whatever perceived imperfection you think you have, and don't doubt God's taste. He made you. He loves what he sees: you.

Dear Lord, I know you're wondering why I don't love myself more. Please help me see myself in your light. Help me not succumb to societal pressures to look a certain way. Help me be content with your holy design for me and find happiness, as did St. Thérèse, in being a little flower among "the splendor of the rose and the whiteness of the lily."[3]

Above all, remind me that my soul deserves far more attention than my hair or figure. The only one I should be comparing myself to isn't found in fashion magazines, on television, or even in my circle of friends. It is you, Holy One, whom I want to be more like. I only have to look as far as the tabernacle to find the source of all beauty and splendor. Amen.

For Your Reflection

• Is there a female media figure you admire not for her physical appearance but for some other quality?
• Read Ephesians 5:1–20. How can you be a better imitator of God?
• Who is one of your favorite saints, and why?

- Not all media promote an unrealistic standard of beauty or objectify women as ornaments instead of human beings. What are some positive media? How can you better support media that uphold human dignity?
- Read Ephesians 3:1–13 and Luke 18:9–14. How can you embrace a healthy humility?

chapter two

Hunger Pangs

When I used to starve myself, eating only scraps of plain lettuce, I was no doubt physically hungry. But almost any preoccupation with food or weight is not just about being hungry or longing to be thinner. Food can be a way of feeding feelings or avoiding them altogether, and weight can be a false measure of self-worth.

Eating too little or too much is often a means of coping with fears and insecurities. In fact, eating disorders, food addictions, and body-image problems are frequently symptoms of a greater disease. We have to uncover the feelings behind our actions to allow real healing to begin.

I learned that being the master of what I ate and of the number on the scale was a way for me to feel "in control" and "good enough." I was convinced that conforming to a certain size would make me more lovable. Losing weight offered hope when the world did not.

My eating disorder relapse occurred in college, after I had suffered a broken heart. I felt as if my world was crumbling. So I turned to controlling my weight as a way of steadying myself.

As my weight dropped, I experienced some relief from my distress. But it was a makeshift Band-Aid that didn't stick for long. And I was always hungry—not only for food but for answers to questions about what I was supposed to do with my life and where, oh, where would I find the love and acceptance I so desperately craved. The feelings of unworthiness I held in the pit of my stomach—these were my true hunger pangs.

Thankfully, I didn't want to tread the same path of starvation and purging I once had. I longed to be healthy again. I knew I could not find love stepping on the scale. So I began my real journey toward healing.

Most women will not induce vomiting or starve themselves to the point of emaciation. But many beautiful, amazing women I know have a warped relationship with food. Many are hungry, starving even, for something other than food.

While some of us don't eat enough, many of us eat more than our healthy share. We have it in our heads that if we fill our stomachs, we'll fill our hearts. We eat beyond satiety. Convenience food is everywhere. We can have our fill anytime. We clean our plates, yet we're still famished—starving for something other than food. We eat and drink, but we're not merry. We do not hunger because we lack food; we hunger because we lack God.

I Scream, You Scream, We All Scream for—God?

It had been one of those days—long on things to do, short on time, energy, and patience. I was very pregnant, and my toddler was cranky. My empathetic preschooler was determined to help me at the grocery store. While her heart was in the right place, a four-year-old can't really lift heavy items out of the cart and put them on the conveyor belt without Mom's help. Meanwhile, my toddler was tightly wrapped around my leg like a boa constrictor. The entire cart-unloading process ended up taking much longer than it should have. Oh, and I had to pee. Badly.

After the grocery store we had to go straight to the pediatrician for my toddler's well-child visit. There I learned that my daughter's iron levels remained low, even after taking a prescription-strength iron supplement, and the pediatrician ordered further testing to rule out any underlying condition. We headed to an off-site lab, where I had to hold my baby girl down and watch her wriggle in pain while the phlebotomist drew blood from her tiny body.

My older daughter stood outside the room whimpering. I peeked out at her, and she was chewing on her shirt, distraught over her sister's crying. I was on the verge of tears too, trying not to show my worry about my daughter and the possibility that her anemia could be a sign of something serious.

When we finally made it back to our car, both of my daughters exploded in despair. I felt hopeless. I knew they needed hugs, but I couldn't offer them my arms while driving.

Then I made an unexpected turn.

My four-year-old instantly noticed that we weren't headed for home. With amazing self-determination she stopped sobbing and asked, "Where are we going?"

"To get ice cream for lunch."

"Ice cream for lunch?"

"Yes."

Both girls clapped their hands. Wow, oh, wow! Spontaneously getting ice cream for lunch was completely out of character for me, but I felt as if we all deserved something out of the ordinary.

After we finished gulping down the ice cream, I felt better—but only temporarily. I was still stressed about my daughter's looming medical test results. (It turned out she was fine.) I realized I was feeding my feelings. I was using ice cream as therapy, instead of turning to God or at the very least my mom or a good friend.

Later that evening as I hovered over the sink, washing our dishes from dinner—which had consisted of healthier fare—I began to wonder what kind of example I had set for my children by finding solace in a bowl of ice cream instead of bringing my anxiety to God.

Life is bountiful, good, fun—and sometimes very, very hard. When the going gets tough, when you feel insecure, anxious, or out of control, it's easy to turn to food for comfort, just as I turned to Ben & Jerry's. Maybe when you feel stressed or sad, you grab a brownie or a bag of potato chips and mindlessly eat. It can't hurt, right?

Maybe not, but it can't help either. Sure, you may feel a temporary numbness while your lips are smacking. But as soon as that last chip is swallowed, you realize that the food is gone but the feelings (and unfortunately the calories) remain.

There's nothing wrong with savoring an occasional indulgence. (I say everyone needs one small piece of dark chocolate a day, and occasionally eating ice cream for lunch as a treat is fine if it's not just to escape stress or the ennui of life.) But let's be careful not to see food as therapy. To prevent emotional eating, ask yourself: What am I really hungry for? Often it is not food.

You may not be physically hungry at all. Maybe you're just feeling frazzled. A quick walk, a call to a friend, or, most important, time spent in prayer would do just as well to soothe your frayed edges. In all the quotidian details of life, train yourself to turn first to Christ. When you seek comfort, turn to the Lord, not your fridge. And even when life is good and you have reason to celebrate, don't fill your glass of wine just yet. First fill your heart with gratitude to God.

Fed by God

We do not live by bread alone—or, as I've had to teach my daughters, we do not live by ice cream alone! Not that food isn't important in our daily lives—Scripture is rich with passages about the importance of gathering around the table to break bread together. God fed his children in the desert with manna raining down from heaven, and the people shared the bountiful blessing of food together (see Exodus 16:4; Psalm 78:24-25). Jesus' first miracle was to transform water into wine—taking something ordinary and making it extraordinary—at the wedding at Cana, where people were gathered to celebrate and to be nourished (John 2:1–11). Jesus later took the simple offering of five loaves of bread and two fish and multiplied it to feed the masses (Matthew 14:13–21). And let's not forget the Last Supper, the first eucharistic banquet, where God's love was made edible (Matthew 26:20–29; Mark 14:17–25; Luke 22:14–20).

Food is surely something to be savored and enjoyed in the company of friends and family as well as a blessing from God. It's also something our bodies need to run properly. But the food itself—at its most basic level—is simply fuel for our bodies. Let's not turn it into something it's not: an idol or a form of therapy.

Once I was sitting in a café and I heard a young woman bemoan the cookie she'd indulged in earlier that day. She spoke as if she'd broken a sacred covenant: Thou shalt not eat "bad" food. Forgive me, Father, for I have sinned—with a cookie. She's not the first woman to berate herself for eating a forbidden food. She's not the only woman to vilify a cookie either. But here's the truth: Food is not your friend, and it's not your enemy either.

Food is neither good nor bad. It's not your confidante, your seducer, your betrayer, or your lover. It's just food. You need to eat to live, but you don't live to eat. Our lives and thoughts should not revolve around when, where, and what our next meal will be.

So how do we put food in its proper place?

We must detach ourselves from food and its power over us and our happiness. This isn't easy, for several reasons.

First, for many of us food has become a sort of god we turn to when we're happy, sad, anxious, or feeling just about anything. Second, in our society food and diet propaganda are everywhere, so it's difficult to not overthink food. We have easy access to food, yet at the same time we're told to cut carbs and other "evil" saboteurs from our meal plan if we want to achieve health.

A lot of us fall into the trap of gulping down everything but real food. We also forget what we knew instinctively as a child: to eat when we're hungry and to stop before we're uncomfortably full.

For today, aim to eat wholesome, healthy foods—like fresh produce and lean protein. Detachment from food doesn't mean deprivation.

At the same time, don't look at the contents of your pantry as evidence of your morality. Fried food and ice cream may not be the best food for your body, but they're not poison, either. "Everything in moderation" is a good rule to follow when it comes to eating.

Detachment may take time; for some of us it may take a lifetime. Likewise, it may be scary to let go of dieting rituals and emotional eating, which have become a way of life for some of us. I've heard several friends remark that an addiction to food is the worst addiction of all, because unlike drugs or alcohol, you can't just quit eating food. Learning to eat mindfully, without suffering from feast or famine, can be as difficult as it would be for an alcoholic to drink three times a day but not get drunk.

But in God, "all things are possible" (Mark 10:27). As someone who's been there, I offer you the hope that you can work day by day, prayer by prayer, to stop allowing food to take the number-one seat in your life. Only God should be sitting there.

One way to put food in its proper place, aside from prayer, is to learn to eat mindfully. Listen to the physical, not emotional, signs that you are hungry, and pay attention to the signals that you are satisfied.

When I was recovering from my eating disorder, I had a hard time eating the right amount. I was tempted either to deprive myself or to treat food as a stolen pleasure. A part of me was in fear of falling into starvation mode again. I had to really work on listening to my body and eating to the point of satiety but not beyond it. (I still have to work at it, in fact.)

I also had to learn not to self-destruct just because I ate a few too many M&Ms. Slowly I've learned to savor small indulgences, to take delight in nuances of flavors, and to appreciate good food and the good company that often comes with it.

If you're craving a cookie, pray first. If you're still craving a cookie, then go on a walk. If that cookie is still on your mind, go ahead and eat one cookie. (But there's no need to devour the whole sleeve of Oreos; they'll still be around tomorrow.) Then let it go. No guilt allowed.

The good news is that there is one kind of food you can never have too much of: the Bread of Life. The best way to fully recover from a food addiction or body-image problem is to fill up on the Lord. Savor his Word. Participate in the Eucharist—spiritual food that fills our mouths and our souls and that encourages us to give thanks rather than focus on what we lack. (*Eucharistia* literally means "to give thanks.")

It is God who offers all the sustenance we'll ever need. He truly is the Bread of Life. He nourishes, and if we "feed" on him instead of food, negative thoughts about our bodies, or a preoccupation with fitness, we will never be hungry. God offers a peace the world—and Ben & Jerry's—cannot give.

Soul Food

Consider this: Your soul—more than your stomach—knows what you really need. On the other hand, your relationship with food may give you insight into your spiritual life. St. John Vianney said, "Do not let us be led by our appetite; we shall ruin our health, we shall lose our soul."[1]

Fasting is a good regimen for some people, though it is dangerous territory for me. In my eating disorder days, I used lenten fasting as subterfuge for my unhealthy eating habits. There was nothing pious about it; rather, it was a part of my sickness.

However, some people find that periodic fasting is very helpful in ripening the fruit of detachment. Hunger pangs remind them that physical hunger is not nearly as strong as hunger for Christ. St. Frances de Sales wrote, "If you are able to endure fasting, you would do well to fast some days besides those which are commanded by the Church. For besides the usual effects of fasting, namely, to elevate the spirit, to keep the flesh in subjection, to exercise virtue, and to acquire a greater reward in heaven, it is a great means to restrain gluttony, and keep the sensual appetites and the spirit subject to the law of the spirit."[2]

Reflect on the following Scripture: "You have sown much, and harvested little; you eat, but you never have enough; you drink, but you never have your fill" (Haggai 1:6). What can you do to be satisfied? No one is ever so empty as when she is full of herself. Look beyond the physical world and start examining your heart and what God—not exercise or food or the right lipstick—can do for you.

After receiving Holy Communion, St. Margaret of Cortona remarked, "My soul is greater than the world since it possesses you, you whom heaven and earth do not contain."[3] You are called to the Lord's table to become that which you receive. Feast on the Eucharist, and have your fill of his goodness. Taste him, and become more like him. As the saying goes, "You are what you eat."

The prophet Amos spoke of a coming famine on the land, "not a famine of bread, nor a thirst for water, but of hearing the words of the LORD" (Amos 8:11). Instead of focusing on your diet—what you should or shouldn't be eating—why not focus your energies on feeding yourself with God's Word? Be sure to share your spiritual helpings with others.

Meditation

What are you hungry for? What does your heart really seek? Peace? Love? A new job? A child? A moment's rest?

The answers to life's problems are not found in your pantry. God is waiting for you to reach out to him. He calls you to eat food because it's delicious and good for you, not because it's a balm for a hurting heart.

When we are empty, God invites us to turn to the one food none of us can live without: the Eucharist. This is the divine food that nourishes our souls. It's the one meal we should never skip. And there's no need for moderation: Jesus is there for the taking.

We should also feed on God's Word. Pope Benedict XVI applied the analogy of eating to "'spiritual reading' of Sacred Scripture," saying it "consists in [poring] over a biblical text for some time, reading and rereading it, ... 'ruminating' on it as the Fathers say and squeezing from it ... all its 'juice,' so that it may nourish meditation and contemplation and, like water, succeed in irrigating life itself."[4]

> *Lord Jesus, make me turn to you first at every turn in life. Remind me to cast my cares onto your strong shoulders and to remember that you can handle the extra weight.*
>
> *Jesus, I am hungry for many things: acceptance, love, truth, happiness, and peace. You tell us, "Whoever comes to me will never be hungry, and whoever believes in me will never be thirsty" (John 6:35, NRSV). I long to sit at your table. Give me your daily bread. Nourish me with your Word. Satisfy my hungry heart with your love. Amen.*

For Your Reflection

• What's your relationship with food like? How could it be better?

- Why do you think so many people eat beyond physical hunger and struggle with maintaining a healthy, balanced diet?
- Ask yourself, "What am I really hungry for?" If you're really struggling, a counselor might be able to help you answer this question. Consider keeping a food journal for a week and writing down not only what you eat but how you feel when you eat it.
- What's one of your favorite foods? Why? Sit down and eat this food with absolutely no distractions. Slowly chew it, savoring its taste. If you start to feel full, stop eating. Take pleasure in your favorite treat, but don't let it control you. Write about the experience of mindfully eating this food.

chapter three

Achieving Real Beauty

Once I found my oldest daughter playing in her toy kitchen, whipping up an interesting dish. In a miniature pot she'd thrown together some plastic carrots, some plastic lettuce, and a Cinderella figurine.

"What are you making?" I asked.

"It's Cinderella stew," she said, stirring the interesting blend of ingredients.

I chuckled, thinking there was something comforting about boiling up Cinderella and all she stands for—beautiful perfection—along with some vegetables.

I'm not sure we have to go as far as poaching Cinderella, but we do have to be careful not to idolize physical beauty. I've often thought about how I want to prevent my daughters from being thrust into a competition to be the fairest of the fair. In fact, I once confessed to my husband that I hoped our daughters would grow up to be plain, or maybe even cute, but not beautiful.

Sure, society makes us think that beauty will give women power, help them get noticed, and give them an advantage in life. However, I've seen far too many beautiful and unhappy girls to think that women should put beauty on a pedestal. The throngs of Hollywood glamour queens spring immediately to mind—women who seem to have it all and end up with eating disorders, in drug rehab programs, or caught up in endless games of marriage roulette.

Why do so many beautiful girls have trouble finding happiness? Here's my theory: Maintaining beauty is too exhausting. Once you have it (or once society says you do), you cling to it, thinking it's all you've got. Your worth becomes so wrapped up in your physical beauty that you'll do anything—starve yourself, resort to plastic surgery—to maintain it.

And yet this kind of beauty isn't something you can hold on to forever. It eventually fades. Botox won't save you. Neither will facelifts. Smooth skin becomes wrinkled and splattered with age spots. Even the firmest of bodies eventually begins to droop. Hair of all shades will end up some variation of gray. In time our faces and bodies won't seem like our own. Physical beauty, while certainly a blessing and not something we should deny or hide if and when we have it, is ephemeral.

While I'm not suggesting all pretty girls are miserable, I've encountered my share of women who look beautiful on the outside but are struggling with some ugly inner demons—from crippling perfectionism to an obsession with looking a certain way. What's worse, they often receive no sympathy from others. When we see beautiful people, we assume they should feel the way they look—beautiful, happy, perfect. If they don't feel that way, we shake our heads and wonder why someone who "has it all" can't be happy.

The opposite often holds true for people who might not be what society would label as physically attractive. Perhaps they are even disfigured. It's easy for us to feel pity toward them and to assume they're carrying oaken crosses, when in reality they might be perfectly at peace and happy with their lives.

Society has taught us to assume a lot based on appearance. It's easy to "size people up" just by looking at them. When we do this, we're guilty of more than jumping to unfair conclusions. We see people not as human beings but as objects.

The Catholic Church is very clear about the dignity of the human person. "The divine image is present in every man," the *Catechism* tells us (*CCC,* #1702), man here referring to the human race, both male and female. We must recognize the worth of each person— from the unborn child to the disabled adult. So start looking at people—including yourself—through Christ's eyes, a lens of love.

As women, we bear a special responsibility when it comes to our appearance. We are part of God's plan for beauty. Just as he made the rose alluring, he made women to be expressions of his love for all that is good and beautiful.

Our beauty gives us power. We have the ability to capture the hearts of others, especially men. Let us attract people with our true beauty and dignity. All of our actions can either give glory to God or misrepresent his truth.

When Satan tempted Eve with the apple, he was saying, "Here, take this. You need this because you're not good enough without it." Society hands us the same types of apples every day. "If you want to get noticed, wear this." "If you want to feel better about yourself, lose some weight." We're right to refuse the apples. We don't need anything. We have everything in God's love. Only when we refuse the apples will we begin to recognize that everyone has worth, and everyone is indeed beautiful.

Beauty That's More Than Skin Deep

Real beauty—and the peace that comes with it—has little to do with a person's appearance. Physical beauty may only be skin deep, but real beauty comes from deep within. It's a cliché, but it's true. Look no further than St. Damien of Molokai for evidence of this.

As I mentioned in the first chapter, most sacred art depicts saints with images that are appealing to the eye. But photos of St. Damien in his later years tell his real story. He is known as the martyr of charity for tending to the physical and spiritual needs of people with leprosy. These people had been shut off from the rest of the world in a government-sanctioned quarantine settlement on the Hawaiian island of Molokai. After devoting nearly two decades of his life to those people, Damien contracted the disease. It showed no mercy but ravaged his body, ripping his skin apart to leave oozing wounds.

And yet St. Damien radiated what is true and beautiful, "the glory of God and…the very stamp of his nature" (Hebrews 1:3). He sacrificed his health, his body, his entire life, out of love for God and others. Even as his physical appearance deteriorated, his spiritual beauty continued to inspire love and respect among the people he served.

This is the kind of beauty we should all strive for. Fortunately, it's a beauty that's not as subjective as physical good looks.

Though physical beauty has always been lauded, there is no universal agreement on what defines it. One person can look at a piece of art and see it as transforming and breathtaking, while someone else can see the same piece as cringe-worthy or too simple to even be considered art. What makes someone physically attractive changes over time and isn't uniform across cultures. Imagine this: Plumpness was once revered, and women were chastised for being too thin. (As a dear friend of mine once commented, maybe we were born in the wrong century!)

But kindness, generosity, and love? These never go out of style. Don't let society define what is beautiful. Leave that up to God.

In his 1994 Letter to Families, Blessed Pope John Paul II wrote, "When we speak about 'fairest love' [described in the Song of Solomon], we are also speaking about beauty: the beauty of love and the beauty of the human being who, by the power of the Holy Spirit, is capable of such love."[1]

Perhaps this is how someone like St. Damien, who experienced great physical suffering as well as disfiguring sores all over his body, could make peace with himself and his life. He was a beautiful human being because of his gift of self, because of the beauty of his generous love.

This also might explain why I always feel gorgeous right after I've had a baby. I surely don't look like a femme fatale—exhausted, sweaty, and clad in a paper gown—but nursing a newborn baby, with my husband by my side, makes me feel just lovely. Maybe it's because I have allowed my body to be used to fulfill God's will, to bring forth new life. Maybe it's because nursing is a gift of self or because having a baby is the closest I've come to witnessing one of God's miracles. Whatever the reason, when I long to feel like a beautiful human being, I sometimes reflect on the moment of one of my children's birth. Such moments show that I am capable of great love.

Mary, Mirror of Perfection
My oldest daughter hasn't cooked up any more Cinderella stew, and in fact, like most little girls, she's drawn to ethereal fairies and pretty princesses. But she's also drawn to another beautiful woman. I once caught her gazing up at a statue of Our Lady before we began to pray a rosary. "Mommy, isn't she pretty?" she said, beaming at her Mother.

"Yes," I said. "She's the most beautiful woman in the world."

Our Blessed Mother is one woman and one type of beauty I do want my girls to imitate: not because she wears fashionable clothes and has lustrous hair, flawless skin, or the body of a siren, but because her soul—her entire being—proclaims the greatness of the Lord (see Luke

1:46). She is "blessed" because she "believed that there would be a fulfillment of what was spoken to her from the Lord" (Luke 1:45).

Mary is a model of what Pope John Paul II referred to as the feminine "genius." For she not only possessed the sublime gifts of "sensitivity for human beings in every circumstance," a receptive heart and
spirit, generosity, and maternity—both in the physical and spiritual
sense—but she also devoted herself to cultivating them.[2] Mary is what
every woman should strive to be: pious, humble, gentle but strong, and
blessed.

As my daughters and I clasped our hands in prayer before this mirror of perfection, I realized that we'll never stop wanting to be beautiful. It's natural for us to want to attract others. The problem is in mis-
taking slenderness or smooth, perfect skin for true beauty. I want my
girls to be beautiful not by society's definition but in God's eyes. I pray
that they and all daughters of God may be as beautiful and lovely and
worthy of roses as the Blessed Mother.

Soul Food

Good skin and flat abs might get you noticed in this world, but God's
more interested in your devotion to him. Proverbs 31 reminds us:
"Charm is deceitful, and beauty is vain, / but a woman who fears the
LORD is to be praised. Give her of the fruit of her hands, and let her
works praise her in the gates" (Proverbs 31:30–31).

Want to know the best beauty secret? Consider Peter's words: Don't
let your beauty rely on "the outward adorning with braiding of hair,
decoration of gold, and wearing of robes, but let it be the hidden person of the heart with the imperishable jewel of a gentle and quiet spirit,
which in God's sight is very precious" (1 Peter 3:3–4). Kindness, gen-
tleness, humility, and freedom from vanity—these are the real marks of
a beautiful woman.

The *Catechism* tells us, "God created the world to show forth and communicate his glory. That his creatures should share in his truth, goodness, and beauty—this is the glory for which God created them" (*CCC*, #319). Notice that God did not create us to parade our physical beauty, if we happen to be blessed with appealing features. Nor are we to focus on our blemishes. Instead, God calls us to lives of truth and goodness—radiant lives that reflect his love, compassion, and mercy.

Forget the great skin or hair. "The 'pure in heart' are promised that they will see God face to face and be like him. Purity of heart is the precondition of the vision of God. Even now it enables us to see according to God, to accept others as 'neighbors'; it lets us perceive the human body—ours and our neighbors'—as a temple of the Holy Spirit, a manifestation of divine beauty" (*CCC*, #2519; see 1 Corinthians 13:12; 1 John 3:2).

To perceive this "divine beauty," we must learn to have "God eyes." We must see people not as objects but as human beings, with souls and with bodies through which they express their souls. Cardinal Joseph Ratzinger, now Pope Benedict XVI, encouraged us to free ourselves "from the impression of the merely sensible, and in prayer and ascetical effort acquire a new and deeper capacity to see, to perform the passage from what is merely external to the profundity of reality."[3] In other words, we must learn to see what our eyes might miss—the beauty that shines from the inside out with the light of Christ.

Consider the words of St. Augustine: "So great is the rational beauty of the human body, and even of the lower and less noble parts, that they are considered pleasant and superior to any other visible form according to the judgment of the spirit of the eyes which are used."[4] Your body—even if it bears scars, flaws, or disfiguring features—is a marvel. The human body is beautiful not simply because of its form but because of its amazing function.

When you smile, for example, twenty facial muscles are at work.[5] And consider the unbelievable endurance of the heart: a muscle that never tires, works twenty-four hours a day, every day, and pumps life-giving blood to a vast highway of blood vessels that has a length of approximately ninety thousand miles—equivalent to the distance you would travel if you went around the earth almost four times.[6]

Just as we may lose some of our physical beauty to age or disease, sin can obscure our inner beauty. Yet while physical beauty cannot be redeemed (without great effort and expense, that is) until the Lord takes our lowly body and glorifies it, our souls can be restored to beauty by God's grace through prayer and the sacrament of confession. What a relief to know that we can remain beautiful so long as we ask for forgiveness and keep God close in our hearts!

Meditation

Many of us long for beauty and find ourselves extolling the charms of full lips, shiny hair, and just the right amount of curve. And why? Because we've been told prettiness will somehow make us better—and more loved. Do we really want to bear the mark of physical beauty? Or do we just want to be loved? Are we longing for good looks or for peace in our hearts?

The next time you have an ugly day, remember this: You are loved. You're also beautiful because God is the Author of beauty. It doesn't matter if you have a zit the size of Mount Kilimanjaro on the tip of your nose or if you're having a really bad hair day. God sees nothing but beauty in you.

God is the perfect artist. Every brush stroke is purposed. For today, give thanks to God for his handiwork. Give God thanks for the lovely creation that is you!

Dear Mary, I want to be like you and to be beautiful in your son's eyes. I want to live a holy life that reflects goodness and truth. Help me look to you as my model of real beauty, and help me be a humble handmaid of the Lord. I want to be modest, to not draw attention to myself with flashy adornments but instead attract others with a kind heart. Don't allow me to get so wrapped up in my physical beauty that I neglect to live a life of beauty—a life that gives to others, a life that says yes to God and bends to his will, a life that lifts up its heart—not just its pretty face—to heaven. Amen.

For Your Reflection

- What makes you feel beautiful? Giving birth? Mastering a new skill? Dancing? Going on a date with your husband? Performing a random act of kindness? Make your own list of "beauty tips." Then commit to choosing at least one of them to do every day.
- How would you define beauty? What are some of the world's most beautiful things (not people) to you? Why?
- Who are some of the most beautiful people you know? What makes them beautiful?
- Read Luke 12:22–34. What steps can you take to be more trusting about what you wear, what you eat, and how you look?
- Proverbs 31:10–31 describes the ideal wife, who "is far more precious than jewels." Whether you are married or single, how can you aspire to be more like her? How can you be more beautiful in God's eyes?

chapter four

Cocreating Life

I was strolling along the Alabama shoreline—holding the hand of my toddler, toting my baby in a sling, and watching my preschooler amble ahead, sifting the sand for shells—when a novel thought hit me, with nearly as much impact as the waves walloping the beach: I am beautiful.

It didn't matter that I hadn't had a shower or that I was tired and probably looked it. It didn't matter that my hair was askew and my face was bare and splotchy. It didn't matter that I hadn't lost all the weight from my most recent pregnancy. I'm sure I resembled a Sasquatch more than a siren from the sea. Yet I felt beautiful. Not glamorous or drop-dead gorgeous, but beautiful all the same.

Beautiful. This was a slippery word for me. The idea that I was beautiful stayed with me about as long as my daughter kept that sand cupped in her hands.

There had been moments when I'd felt pretty—like on my wedding day, or when I dressed up to go out on a date with my husband—but I rarely could hold onto the feeling. Insecurity about my appearance—how awful I looked in my clothes or how full my face looked in pictures—was never far away. The beach, in particular, was always a land mine of body-image blasts. While I was supposed to feel carefree, with my feet on the warm sand and my eyes on the ocean, as soon as I slipped into a swimsuit, I'd immediately become encumbered by every lump of my flesh.

Yet there I was on the beach, comfortable in my own skin, even though there was a bit more of it after having my third child. I could walk along in a swimsuit and not worry about sucking in my stomach or taming my wild hair.

It took having three children to make me fully aware and appreciative of my beauty. This is the kind of beauty that has little to do with aesthetics and everything to do with strength and dignity. Motherhood, like nothing else, should make us aware of our femininity, our power to nurture and to love. It assures us of our power to look beyond ourselves, our own needs, and our outer shell of hairstyles and curves, to see glimpses of what it means to give, to lay down our lives for others, to be like Christ.

Making Peace With Your "Mom Bod"

If you've been blessed with bearing a child, you, too, may have struggled with the changes in your body after the baby was born. If not, you may find parallels in your own life—perhaps with changes due to age or injury or surgery. I haven't always appreciated my body's strength. When I noticed a set of stretch marks after the birth of my first child, to say I wasn't pleased is an understatement. I became rather obsessed with these new marks of motherhood. The lines eventually faded, and thankfully, so did most of my postpartum body angst. Maternity taught me what nothing else could: that my physical appearance was not the keystone of my identity and that seeing it change and soften should be a source of pride, not stress.

Many women receive the gift of fertility. Other women find their maternity through adoption. Still others become spiritual mothers, caring for those whom God puts on their path. Whatever our vocation, it should be obvious that our bodies are not objects to be picked apart. Even if we bear some physical signs of motherhood, such as stretch marks, a scar from a C-section, or softer forms, we are not broken or in need of repair. Our bodies are God-designed instruments that help us live our vocations as wives, mothers, and caregivers.

Pregnancy, motherhood, and certainly time will change a woman's body. Skin loosens; gravity does its part. Instead of seeing these inevitable physical changes as flaws, why not see them as sacrificial signs that you are using your body for what God intended you to— to be a wife, to be a nurturer, to cocreate life with God?

As moms we have a responsibility to be healthy role models for our children—to eat well, exercise, and take care of ourselves—and it's perfectly reasonable to want to shed your baby weight, even if your youngest "baby" is headed off to college. But the key is to remain realistic and to make being healthy rather than being slimmer your priority. Try to focus on health and happiness, not the number on the scale or a smaller jean size.

After I have a baby, I concentrate on balanced eating and exercise, even if all I have time for is a family game of tag. I also remind myself to be patient. Most normal women—as in all of us who don't have the luxury of personal trainers, nutritionists, and chefs at our service— should expect it to take nine months to a year to shed the baby weight. Embrace healthy habits, but don't become a slave to the scale.

Even if you never shed all your pregnancy weight, remind yourself of the ample beauty found in your maternity. We are stronger because of our children—the babes to whom we give birth, the kids we lift, the errant toddlers and teenagers we pursue. There's great demand for our energy. Let's not waste it by punishing ourselves.

Let's also not waste our lives trying to hold on to the illusion of control. As a mom, I sometimes feel powerless. I cannot control the number of hours (minutes!) I spend sleeping. I cannot always control my children's behavior, try as I might. The temptation then is to get control where I can, to whip my body into submission.

When I feel that I'm lacking as a mother, it's temping to become a master of my weight. I can deprive myself of calories. If I eat too much, or if the number on the scale gets stuck at an "unreasonable" number, I can skip breakfast or exercise longer and harder. Not surprisingly, eating disorders frequently crop up during motherhood. We may begin pursuing the look of a "yummy mummy," but what we really long for is control.

When you feel you're at your wits' end—wondering why your children don't listen, why they can't get along, when they're going to grow up—take a deep breath and hand them over to God. He loves them more than you do. You're not in control; you never were. But God is, and he's a good, loving parent who knows what he's doing.

See Yourself Through Your Family's Eyes

After the birth of my third baby, my stomach stayed soft for a long time. I mentioned something to my husband (poor guy has to deal with my body angst) about how my broad hips and fuller form weren't going away. "Good," he said. "I like it when you look like a woman."

Most husbands see our womanly forms as beautiful. What can become unattractive are our own constant diatribes against our bodies.

Neither are our children concerned with our body shape or the amount of cellulite on our thighs. We are beautiful in their eyes because we are their mothers. We don't have to be a pretty "something." Being *someone*—a mother who cares for them—is enough.

If family isn't enough reason for you to love your body, consider this: God loves us with an even deeper unconditional love.

When I became a parent, my home took on a new look—a cluttered, smudgy kind of look. I crave order, but for several years we shared Sardinesville with three little ones, making a *House-Beautiful* kind of home next to impossible. There were closets brimming with little girl dresses. Dolls and stuffed animals frequently reclined on the couch. Our food-flinging babies added a Technicolor flare to the beige carpet in our dining area.

Still, this was our home—the place where my middle child took her first teetering steps, where we arrived with our third bundle of joy, and where my oldest started to read. I didn't want to erase all the signs that kids lived there. I have the same mind-set about the larger home where we now live. I'm not managing a museum; I'm raising a family.

Similarly, my body is my children's first home. So how can I expect it to remain the same after God invited me to share in the miracle of new life? I have cocreated life, and that creation has taken its toll physically.

I get very sick during pregnancy. Each time I find myself awash in nausea, I remind myself that something miraculous is going on within me: A little human being is there, and God, great sculptor that he is, is shaping and molding my child's features. My body may never be the same again, but neither will my life. My girth may widen, but so does my heart.

My baby spits up on our carpet, my toddler drops berries on the same carpet, and the budding artist of the family adds her finishing touches when she accidentally lets a wet paintbrush slide off the table. I take to my knees and scrub the floor, just as I care for my body, recognizing it as a reflection of God's great love for me. But I don't expect perfection.

I've earned my mothering stripes in the form of stretch marks—reminders that God has given me children and souls to nurture. Surely they and a few extra pounds are a small price to pay for the sublime gift of motherhood.

Mothers, let's make a pact to embrace our femininity, our maternity —rounder hips and all. Let's remind ourselves that pursuing thinness and prebaby jeans has no eternal value at all, but raising children and doing good works do. Beam at your children, and know that they think you are beautiful. Because you are.

Soul Food

Take a prolife stance. Celebrate your children and the body being a mother has blessed you with.

Berating your maternal body, on the other hand, is a way of accepting the all-too-common worldview that children are burdens instead of blessings. When you're tempted to rebuke your body, hold close the words of St. Jean Baptist De La Salle: "I will often consider myself as an instrument which is of no use except in the hands of the workman."[1] Motherhood makes you an instrument in God's hands.

"Take delight in the LORD, and he will give you the desires of your heart" (Psalm 37:4). Delight in the Lord and the gift of motherhood instead of delighting in "skinny jeans." Do not allow physical beauty to be the pillar of your identity. You are a woman. You are a mother. You are a wife. You are first and foremost a child of God. That makes you lovely in every way.

Blessed Pope John Paul II held a high esteem for mothers and thanked them personally in his Letter to Women in June 1995: "Thank you, women who are mothers! You have sheltered human beings within yourselves in a unique experience of joy and travail. This experience makes you become God's own smile upon the newborn child, the one who guides your child's first steps, who helps it to grow and who is the anchor as the child makes its way along the journey of life."[2]

Remember the Proverbs 31 woman. She is not preoccupied with earthly things and having a flawless appearance; she has the physical strength necessary to meet the sometimes exhausting demands of being a wife and caretaker of other souls. Like her, we need the grit and grace of God to tote diaper bags, stacks of library books, our kids' athletic gear, and all the other physical loads that being a mother sometimes piles on us. Ask God for the strength to carry out your maternal duties.

Motherhood sometimes requires Herculean strength (think labor). When you find yourself lagging, turn to St. Paul for inspiration. He encourages us to have the tenacity of an athlete by keeping our eyes set on God. If we make God the center of our lives and turn to him frequently throughout the day—when we're enjoying motherhood and when it's leaving us feeling run down—we will be able to run in a way that gets us and our families the prize of heaven (see 1 Corinthians 9:24–27).

St. John Vianney said, "Here is a rule for everyday life: Do not do anything which you cannot offer to God."[3] Try to see mothering and the changes it brings to your physical body as an offering to God. In this way your stretch marks, broader hips, and aching back and arms become gifts to him.

Every time you make love to your husband, carry an infant in your womb, nurse a baby, or hold an older child until your arms ache, you say, "This is my body which is given for you" (Luke 22:19). Jesus sacrificed his body to redeem ours. Let us lay down our own bodies (and our unrealistic dreams of slimmer hips and taut abs) for our families.

Consider the words of Elizabeth to Mary: "Blessed is the fruit of your womb" (Luke 1:42). Christ doesn't grow in our womb, but he does dwell in our souls. And many of our wombs are sacred places where God's handiwork is knit together. Pray a Hail Mary, and be grateful for the fruit of your womb—and of your life—that God has blessed you with.

Meditation

When we praise God and give him thanks, we usually count our blessings, such as our family, job security, health, or even a beautiful day. But how often do we thank him for our bodies?

Have you ever considered the miracle of your fingers—how they can pick up a pen and write a letter to a loved one or make a small child feel secure by enclosing her small hand? What about your breasts— God's design for completely nourishing your children from your body? Or your heart—a strong muscle that works day and night and provides a soothing symphony for a child in your womb?

Your body is a miracle to be praised. So start praising it.

Dear Lord, thank you for the gift of motherhood. Thank you for the miracle and mystery of new life and for inviting me to cocreate with you. Maker of all things, help me love the way you have molded my body for motherhood, just as I love the way you formed my children in my womb. Help me see my physique as an instrument to do your work—to bring life into the world and to nurture that life. Give me the eyes to appreciate my wider hips for carrying tired children and my softer tummy for pillowing their heads.

Use my children to shape me into your image, Lord. Use my pregnancies as means to grow in sacrificial love. Use my children's clinging arms to make me gentler. Use their sweet smiles to make me more aware of my blessings. Use their nocturnal cries to make me more compassionate.

Lord, use my body, my soul, my entire being, not only to be a better physical and spiritual mother but also to do your will. I am beautiful in every way because of you. Amen.

For Your Reflection

• What qualities do you admire most about your mom or another mother figure in your life?

• What qualities do you think your children love the most about you?

• How has motherhood changed the way you see your body?

• What kinds of qualities should a good mother possess?

• Think about your body's accomplishments since you became a mom. Did you make it through labor? Have you nursed a child? Can you lug around a diaper bag and a thirty-pound tot? Can you toss the football with your teenage children? You're a mom. How does that make you physically strong? How does it make you spiritually strong?

chapter five

Like Mother, Like Daughter

After I gave birth to my first healthy daughter, I wasn't overly concerned with my weight or how I looked. I felt strong and capable after having made it through hours of labor. I was content to just hold my new baby. I was in awe of her as she nursed on the milk my body made miraculously. Motherhood suited me well. I was happy, content, and too busy taking care of my newborn to worry about my weight.

Unfortunately, my idyll didn't last.

One morning when my baby was several months old, I was getting dressed and noticed my rounder self in my bedroom mirror. Who was this lumpy woman? Where did the athletic, toned girl I used to be run off to? I tried to look away, but I couldn't stop dismembering my body as if it was a broken-down machine to be dismantled and tweaked. The mirror seemed to taunt me, and all the relics of my unhealthy body image came rushing back like an avalanche of hate.

When I discovered I was having a little girl, I immediately made a promise to avoid talking about my weight and looks and to never berate myself physically or otherwise in her presence. I didn't want my daughter to grow up hating her body. Yet there I was, wrapped up in bad thoughts about this new body and longing for the old one. It hurt to hurl hate at my body again, but even worse, it hurt to think I was already failing my daughter.

Pretty Is as Pretty Does

Thankfully, as he does so often, God gave me a wake-up call that forced me to take a good hard look at something other than my post-partum figure.

One day I was staring at my baby's naked form and admiring all of her dimples and rolls. She grinned at me, looking up with bright eyes. Something about that innocent smile crushed me. I began to cry as I realized that for the first time in my life, my body angst hurt not only me but also my daughter. Each time I punished myself for not being thin enough, each time I shed tears over stretch marks, each time I stood in front of the mirror to berate my body, I was failing to be a healthy role model.

It was time for a body-image makeover. I needed to stop putting my body on the dissection table to pick apart its flaws. I had more to offer the world than skin. I had to be mindful of what I said about looks, for I now had a captive audience.

I shifted my focus from my body to my baby's body. How was she growing and changing? I marveled at her tiny toes and the perfect curve of her ear, which gently wiggled as she nursed. I kissed her soft, round belly. It was far more fun to count her rolls than to obsess over mine. Day by day I pushed aside negative thoughts about how I looked.

As I've grown into motherhood and faced several more pregnancies and the postpartum mushiness that comes with bearing children, I've realized my physical imperfections have no power over my children's love for me. My children love me because of what I do, not because of how I might look in a little black dress. They love me because I feed them, counsel them, cuddle with them, wrestle with them, and tend to their every need.

Fat doesn't seem to bother babies. Their dimply thighs don't keep them from cruising toward whatever catches their curious eyes. They don't care if their mothers are round, either. I'd even go so far as to wager that some babies prefer to rest upon a softer mama. My grandma remembers trying to comfort one of her babies when a pleasantly plump friend took the fussing child and pressed his teary face against her ample bosom. The baby stopped crying immediately, and the friend remarked, "Nothing likes a bone except a dog."

Babies see beauty and love as one. The mother who loves them— anyone who loves them—is beautiful. I want it to stay that way in my family. I want my daughters to recognize that worth runs much deeper than a dress size.

If God blesses my daughters with loveliness, I want them to be grateful but to remember that it's what's beyond skin that's really important—their passions, their brains, their sensitivity, and most important, their souls. I certainly don't want them growing up think- ing that looking like a supermodel is what will make them happy.

While I know I can't shelter my daughters from all the pains and disappointments life has to offer, I can show them that being a strong, capable, beautiful, and healthy woman has little to do with correcting rounder hips, a big nose, saggy skin, or any other perceived body imperfection. My children will have enough societal pressures to over- come as they grow into womanhood—from the temptation to wear immodest clothing to the desire to look like pin-thin actresses. The last thing they need is a self-deprecating mom. What they *do* need is a mom who models healthy eating, who moves her body for the joy of it, and who has made peace with herself and her body.

Let Girls Be Girls

What my daughters need above all is a mother who sees her femininity as a gift, not something to be hidden or ashamed of and not a source of weakness. Being a woman is indeed a rich gift, for "[the woman] represents God from whom comes our help" (*CCC*, #1605; see Genesis 2:18–25). The Church, in fact, believes that, because of their special gifts of love, generosity, sensitivity, and self-giving, women have the power to transform into places of love not only our homes but also the world beyond.

We have to look no further than Mary for proof of how our daily decisions and actions can have far-reaching effects. Because of her faith, because of her saying yes to God, and because of her natural ability to bear children, this ordinary woman became a mother to God himself and is forever linked to the salvation of the entire human family. She is woman as God intends: someone who uses her spiritual and physical gifts to accomplish God's will.

In his Letter to Women, Blessed Pope John Paul II wrote:

> Perhaps more than men, women *acknowledge the person*, because they see persons with their hearts. They see them independently of various ideological or political systems. They see others in their greatness and limitations; they try to go out to them and *help them*. In this way the basic plan of the Creator takes flesh in the history of humanity and there is constantly revealed, in the variety of vocations, that *beauty*— not merely physical, but above all spiritual—which God bestowed from the very beginning on all, and in a particualar way on women.[1]

Likewise, in Scripture Jesus treats the women he encounters with great love and respect. Jesus chose to reveal that he was the Messiah to a woman at a well (see John 4: 7–42). He loved the sisters Martha and Mary and appreciated the hospitality they offered (John 11:5; 12:1–8). Mary Magdalene was the first eyewitness to the risen Christ as well as the first to bear witness of the Resurrection to the apostles (John 20:11–18).

We must help our girls recognize the strengths they possess as women made in the image of God. How?

First, by helping them distinguish Mary as a model of all womanhood. If they follow her lead and allow themselves to be handmaids of the Lord, serving God and his will, then they will be beautiful and holy, without blemish.

Likewise, we need to let our girls be, well, girls. My daughters love to watch me get ready for a date night with my husband. I remember the first time one of them wanted to powder her nose and gloss her lips. At first I balked at her request. She was only two, after all, too young to think about looks or makeup. But then I realized that she wasn't thinking about those things at all. She was thinking about being like her mommy. She was thinking about being a girl. There's a difference.

We're not protecting our daughters if we forbid makeup, eschew fashionable hairstyles, or wear dowdy clothes. The feminine form is beautiful. Sure, we don't want to hide behind makeup or wear immodest clothing to draw attention to ourselves. But there's nothing wrong with wanting to accent our femininity.

What's more, accenting your natural beauty is a gift to your husband. On most days I don't wear much makeup, but I always give my eyelashes a quick swipe of mascara before my husband comes home. My eyes are his favorite feature, and it makes me feel lovely (and human!) to accent them just a little bit, especially if my primary activity of the day involved annihilating toxic diaper waste.

It's important for our daughters as well as our sons to see us value our beauty for the sake of our spouses. Now when I primp, I gladly hand my daughters makeup brushes (usually with nothing on them), which they feather along their cheeks. They imitate me and smack their lips. They like to brush their honey-hued hair. I spritz a cloud of perfume, and we all dance in its mist.

"You look beautiful," my daughters tell me as I twirl in a frothy skirt. Thank God, I'm finally starting to believe them.

Daddy's Little Girls

As my daughters' mother, I have an important—sacred—responsibility to teach them about real beauty and to help them appreciate their femininity. However, I'm careful not to underestimate their father's role in raising them to have healthy body images.

I know several women who have suffered from eating disorders as well as negative body image throughout their lives. I asked each of them what she thought might have contributed to her body angst. While they were careful to not excuse themselves of all blame, several women talked about how their fathers were overly critical of their or their mothers' looks. One friend told me that her father always looked at her as if she was an object and not a person. Other fathers would frequently remark on the food their daughters ate.

While a father might not be intentionally trying to hurt his daughter and may even be trying to protect her, saying things like, "Are you really going to wear that?" can inflict damage. It's better to discuss modesty and beauty in God's terms. "You are beautiful and sacred because you are a child of God. There's no need to draw attention to yourself with revealing clothing. If you don't want to be treated like an object, don't display your body like an object. Remember, my beloved, that modesty protects the mystery that is you."

We women have to encourage the men in our lives (including our sons!) to treat our daughters, as well as all females, with respect. Men can help young women see that their dignity comes from their being, not from their level of attractiveness. Dads need to treat their daughters like princesses, even if their girls don't "look" the part.

Physical affection is very important. Encourage the father of your daughters to give plenty of hugs. A girl who is blossoming physically still needs affection from Dad.

Of course, as my parents can attest, both Mom and Dad can do nearly everything "right" and still have a daughter who sees herself as ugly or unworthy. That's when we must fall to our knees and pray for our children and release them into God's loving care. Because as hard as it is to fathom, God loves our children even more than we do.

Raising Healthy Women
As the mom of several daughters, I'm passionate about helping them embrace a healthy love for their bodies and selves by conveying positive, uplifting messages about weight, food, beauty, and overall health. Here are a few more practical tips I try to embrace with my own family, to help raise healthy women who value themselves as God's treasures.

• Be selective in the media you choose to consume, because your kids are looking over your shoulder. In addition, discussing media images and stereotypes is important. For example, remind older children that media often portray an unrealistic physical ideal. Sit down with your children and flip through a popular fashion magazine. Discuss the women's figures. Point out pictures of models representing so-called chic fashion labels and ask, "Do these women really look like strong women, women who take care of themselves?" For comparison, look at images of Our Blessed Mother and other saints you admire, and remind children that these holy people are the epitome of real beauty.

• Make meals a family affair. Eating should not be a solitary pursuit; we are meant to break bread together. Although eating every meal together as a family may not be feasible, especially as children grow older, make sure you eat at least one meal almost every day together. Invite your children to help prepare meals as well.

• During your meals, talk about your day and your faith. Consider discussing healthy food choices and why "real" food—rather than processed food made in a factory—is the best type of fuel for our bodies. But don't make mealtime a battleground. Don't force children to eat something they don't like or to eat when they're not hungry. Children are intuitive eaters, and we can mess them up if we force them to clean their plates or to eat only by the clock rather than according to their physical hunger.

• Teach children that their bodies are not ornamental objects. Here you're bucking what society would have your children believe. Our bodies are homes for the Holy Spirit. Our dignity is found not in the curves of our bodies, but in our very being. We are beautiful because we are sons and daughters of God, not because we look a certain way.

• To this end, be careful about always telling girls that they look pretty or even that their clothes are beautiful. Instead say, "Good job picking out your outfit," or, "You sure do have strong legs. I can't believe how far you can run."

• Don't put too much emphasis on what a young girl chooses to wear (provided it's modest and appropriate for her age) or how she likes to do her hair. I used to tell my little ones that their outfit didn't match or that their hair looked silly in a side ponytail, but then I realized I was inadvertently placing too much emphasis on their appearance. Does it really matter if she wears a polka dot skirt with a floral top, or if she sports ragamuffin hair as she plays around the house?

• Go shopping with your daughter, and gently guide her in making good choices. Encourage children to choose clothes that are comfortable and modest yet chic. There are such things!

Many women opt for form over function. A woman might choose to wear snazzy heels all day long and end up nursing blisters and a sore back. Clothes and shoes can be pretty and feminine without being painful to wear and overly revealing. Beauty often lies in the mystery of the female form. There's no need to hide in a potato sack, but our daughters don't need to flaunt their bodies or subject themselves to pain to get noticed. No matter how they're dressed, they are always worthy of God's attention.

• Give your child some control. Children often feel powerless, and this can lead them to find areas in their lives that they can control—such as eating or not eating.

I have a friend who is determined to give her daughter choices, because as a young girl she felt that she had very little control over anything. A binge made her feel out of control, while a purge was a powerful release that led her to feel as if she was in charge. She suffered from bulimia for years.

This woman gives her daughter some control over what she puts into her mouth. "Do you want an apple or grapes for a snack?" She also gives her other opportunities to make choices in the course of the day, such as choosing her outfit and deciding whether to complete her homework before or after dinner.

But while we're at it, we must also teach our children that a lot of what happens to us is out of our control. It's during these times that we must turn to God for solace and put our trust in him.

Soul Food

When the going gets tough, encourage your children to pray: "Trust in the LORD with all of your heart…. It will be healing to your flesh and refreshment to your bones" (Proverbs 3:5, 8). Although we want hap-piness for our children, life isn't always a ball, and we're not guaranteed a happily ever after. It's up to us to teach children about how grace and faith—more than a magical gown or fairy godmother—will help us navigate life's challenges.

Women in particular often focus too much on their hair, their weight, and their clothing, but life is rich even when we have a bad hair day. To reiterate this, meditate on this Scripture passage with your daughters: "Do not be anxious about your life, what you shall eat or what you shall drink, nor about your body, what you shall put on. Is not life more than food, and the body more than clothing?" (Matthew 6:25).

Remind your girls to "put on then, as God's chosen ones, holy and beloved, compassion, kindness, lowliness, meekness, and patience.... And over all these put on love, which binds everything together in per-fect harmony" (Colossians 3:12, 14). Love is what we really should be "wearing" every day.

Whisper to your daughter, "God loves all things that exist and loathes nothing that he has made, for he would not have made any-thing if he hated it" (see Wisdom 11:24). Tell them—no matter how old they are—that you and God their Creator love them just the way they are.

Help your daughters see that being feminine is part of what makes them unique and treasured. Our daughters don't need to eschew pretty, girly things in order to appear strong. In *Mulieris Dignitatem*, Pope John Paul II's Apostolic Letter on the Dignity and Vocation of Women, the pope warned against the masculinization of women: "[W]omen must not appropriate to themselves male characteristics contrary to their own feminine 'originality.' There is a well-founded fear that if they take this path, women will not 'reach fulfillment,' but instead will deform and lose what constitutes their essential richness."[2]

Meditation

The older your daughter gets, the more you start seeing pieces of yourself in her. Some of the pieces are smooth and beautiful, like the way she brings you flowers just as you bring her meals. But sometimes the pieces are imperfect, rough shards. And yet your child remains lovable in your eyes. She is human, of course, but she always, always deserves love. It is this realization that makes it easier to love yourself and to remember that Christ sees the good in all of us.

Your children are God's children. And so are you. You belong to God, who loves you best and most. God has entrusted you with the responsibility of raising and loving your children. At times it's daunting to have your child's well-being placed in your care. But with God as your helpmate, you're up to the task.

As your child sleeps, gently kiss her on the forehead. Watch your child, and listen to her breathing, her soft sighs. Then whisper this prayer: "Lord, I hand over my child to you. You are her true parent; I am only a guardian. Help me to love her the best I can, and when I falter, please fill in the gaps."

Dear Mary, my children are wonderful gifts. I love being their mother, but sometimes I'm afraid. Be a mother to me now as I care for my children, protect them, and guide them. Give me the strength and grace for the work that lies ahead, as I teach my children to fashion themselves in your son's image.

Our Lady of Consolation, please be my strength if and when I must watch my children suffer. Sweet Mary, I offer myself and my children to you, so that your son may accomplish in us his holy designs. Amen.

For Your Reflection

• We are all God's handiwork (see Ephesians 2:1–10), and we have been called to give him glory and to please him with the gifts he has given us (Romans 12:1–8). How can you help your daughters and sons become whom God wants them to be?

• Part of a mother's job is to train her children in healthy habits. How are you going about this? Is there room for improvement? How can you encourage your children to make healthy choices?

• How are you a good role model for your children in terms of maintaining a healthy body image? How can you improve?

• How can you help your children discover their talents and their personal uniqueness?

• Think about each of your children (your sons too), and write down three qualities you love about each. Share your thoughts with each of your children, and then look him or her in the eye and say, "I love you just the way you are."

chapter six

Aging Gracefully

One of the most beautiful women I know is my ninety-year-old grand-mother. She's as wrinkled as a raisin, and her thin hair is the muted color of oatmeal. She jokes that she knows God must be merciful, because as your skin begins to sag, you lose your vision too, so you don't notice the flaws so much!

My grandmother has no qualms about admitting she needs hearing aides. When you ask her (loudly), "How do you feel?" she replies, laughing and with a twinkle in her liquid blue eyes, "Old."

Nana's age is not a handicap or a source of angst. It is her joy, and this is what makes her beautiful. She is well-worn and creased because, she will tell you, she has lived a long, fruitful life, including raising nine children. She's been around long enough to hold great-grandchildren. She prayed to St. Joseph as her husband of almost sixty years slipped into God's care.

To Nana, wrinkles aren't something you're punished with; they're something you earn, God willing. Although she admits that sometimes it's difficult to be aware of your body growing feeble and deteriorating physically, prayer reminds her that every day is a gift to be unwrapped and lived.

Last Christmas my eye caught hers, and she smiled at me. A herd of grandkids and great-grandkids were gathered at her feet. "I'm so damn lucky," she whispered. I noticed that her eyes were starting to glisten with tears. I squeezed her hand and said, "We're very lucky too."

Nana's not usually an overly sentimental person. My dad and his siblings joke about the few photos documenting their childhood. Nana saw them as unnecessary clutter, for she had the memories. Why would she need pictures to prove a baby smeared spaghetti all over his face?

When I think of the saying "Age before beauty," an image of my old, crinkly grandmother pops up almost immediately. I see so much more than the signs of old age in her. She possesses an ageless, almost supernatural beauty that comes from leading a life of getting to know God better. She's living proof that gray hair is "a crown of glory...gained in a righteous life" (Proverbs 16:31).

Nana doesn't fix her gaze on her age; she's too busy looking ahead to the age to come—the promise of eternity and a new, glorified body in union with Christ. Her faith, her goodness, and her acceptance of her mortal body holding an immortal soul are what make her lovely.

Spend time with your mother, grandmothers, or other older women you know and respect. Like my grandmother, they'll help teach you that age (and I'd like to add wisdom) most definitely comes before physical beauty. We earn our marks in life, so why spend a fortune trying to erase them?

No matter how many years we have under our belts, we will never have enough to prepare us for the heavenly kingdom. Even St. Katharine Drexel, who founded the Sisters of the Blessed Sacrament, said, "Oh, how far I am at eighty-four years of age from being an image of Jesus in his sacred life on earth!"[1] We cannot be "holy enough" without God. Let's invite him to clean us up. Let's open ourselves to his goodness and grace. A good skin cream might make our skin glisten, but only God can make our souls shine.

Embracing the Sands of Time

Seeing my grandmother as beautiful is one thing, but being OK with losing my own youth is another thing altogether. I haven't struggled with it much yet. (Perhaps I've been too consumed with the size of my hips to even notice the smile lines creeping onto my face.)

I know women who haven't even hit the thirty-year mark but have already started to talk about plastic surgery, Botox injections, and the best anti-aging secrets. Why do they fear age instead of seeing it as a gift? Human beings don't have "sell by" dates. Our dignity does not decrease with age. We should hope our wisdom might increase with it, though.

When I was in high school, a classmate died in a car crash. She was my first brush with death, so I remember the details of her wake and funeral vividly. I can still see the image of her in her casket—so perfect, so beautiful, frozen in time, with her flawless skin and soft, long hair like corn silk framing her serene face.

It surprises me how often I think of this classmate, her untimely death, and her youthful beauty. I wonder how she would feel about young reality stars who undergo countless surgical procedures and end up looking as pretty and plastic as Barbie.

I have no problem with using a good face cream and slathering on the sunblock to protect my skin. I'll brush my hair and condition it and move my body to keep it strong and limber. But I refuse to fear aging.

Tomorrow may bring aches and pains, gray hair, and crow's-feet. Tomorrow may bring heartache. Tomorrow I may feel a whole lot younger than I look. But tomorrow—every single day I wake up—is one day I'm gifted with living on this earth.

Let's not waste the years God gives us fearing our mortality. We are not of this world. Like money and fame, physical beauty and youth are worldly pursuits. When we are blessed with them, we should rejoice, but let's not build a life around pursuing attractiveness and fighting aging. Physical beauty is here today and gone tomorrow, and tirelessly working to maintain it does nothing to better our souls. While our faith tells us that with God's mercy we will find peace in the afterlife, let us work to find peace in this one. Peace be with you.

Soul Food

When you're feeling old, take the focus off of you. Catholic convert Dorothy Day is a great example for us. In her old age this modern-day saint grew haggard and wrinkled like the rest of us, but she didn't allow vanity to distract her from continuing the Catholic Worker Movement and fighting against poverty, racism, and violence.

Day, who was around seventy-five at the time, wrote in her diary, "We love God as much as the one we love the least."[2] How much love do you have for yourself—and for God—if you bemoan the real and perceived signs of aging? Embrace the wisdom of Day, and accept and love yourself, no matter your age.

Just think how many souls could be brought to Christ, how many lives touched, if we chose to wage a war against injustices rather than fight against our own flesh. Stop thinking about your outer shell—which will crack no matter how hard you try to keep it from breaking—and get out there and help others.

Consider the wisdom of St. Rita of Cascia: "The more we indulge in soft living and pampered bodies, the more rebellious they will become against the spirit."[3] Pursuing the elusive fountain of youth or desiring to fit a certain human standard of beauty can lead to costly self-indulgences. An obsession with a certain physical ideal can distract you from the "shape" of your soul, which will endure for all eternity.

When your body starts to flounder with age, remember this: "The Lord Jesus Christ…will change our lowly body to be like his glorious body" (Philippians 3:21).

Our physical selves—even if we work very hard to take good care of our bodies—will someday fail us. We'll grow older. We'll get sick. We may even suffer chronic pain.

Elisabeth Leseur (1866–1914) was a French housewife who lived a holy life despite frequent physical suffering. On a particularly painful day, she wrote in her journal, "What a great thing the soul is, and how distinct from and independent of the body! In depression and physical pain, when our poor mental faculties share the lassitude of the body, the soul is still free and continues to live its own life, and upheld by a force that it knows to come from above, it dominates the body and keeps it in its place."[4]

Elisabeth offered her sufferings for the conversion of her atheist husband. He discovered her journal after her death, eventually came back to the Church, and later became a priest.

Your soul is free from physical pain and aging. What a gift to have this imperishable entity that God makes resplendent and beautiful.

Consider the words of St. Ignatius of Loyola:

> Man is created to praise, reverence, and serve God our Lord, and by this means to save his soul. All other things on the face of the earth are created for man to help him fulfill the end for which he is created.... Therefore we must make ourselves indifferent to all created things, in so far as it is left to the choice of our free will and is not forbidden. Acting accordingly, for our part, we should not prefer health to sickness, richness to poverty, honor to dishonor, a long life to a short one. And so in all things we should desire and choose only those things that will best help us attain the end for which we are created.[5]

I'd add that we should not prefer beauty or youth to plainness, age, or even ugliness. Ask yourself this: Is pursuing youth a means of serving Christ? You know the right answer. You are a child of God, and you will always be a child of God, no matter how old you are.

St. Anthony of Padua, who is the patron saint not only of lost things but also of the elderly, reminds us, "The life of the body is the soul; the life of the soul is God."⁶ We get our life from God. Let's allow this life to flow through us to others. This is the beauty we can exude at any age.

Meditation

Not another wrinkle! Is that a gray hair I see? Why is my skin sagging?

Aging is inevitable, and it doesn't always look pretty. We may not be as visually appealing on the outside as we once were. This is the order of nature, and we cannot eschew it. We come from the dust, and we will return to the dust (see Genesis 2:7; 3:19). That's the bad news.

Here's the good news: Growing old does not make us unlovable. God's time is not our own. God knew us and loved us long before we were babies with soft, perfect skin; his love does not stop as we grow—it grows with us.

And there's more. Our aim is not to live in these decaying bodies forever but to live with God in eternal life. Our bodies—wrinkles and all—will pass away. In the evening of life, if all goes well, you'll trade in the body you have now for "a new look" that will be like Jesus' "glorious body" (Philippians 3:21).

Relinquish control. You cannot stop the sands of time. Grow old gracefully by living a life of grace and trusting in God's perennial love for you.

Dear Lord, thank you for each year with which you bless me. I know it might be difficult to see my appearance change with age, yet with your grace I will not fight growing old but embrace it as a sign of your blessing. Purge me of my vanity; help me to be like a fine wine and to age well, growing more beautiful with time.

Finally, lead me to increase not only in age but in wisdom, grace, and goodness. And even as my body grows old, keep my spirit young, and allow me to come to you with a childlike trust in your providence in my life. Amen.

For Your Reflection

• We can learn much from those who have gone before us. Consider how grandparents approach their grandchildren. Most grandparents do not fret over spilled milk or sticky hands. They prefer hugging to scolding. They seem to have learned to not "sweat the small stuff." What can veteran moms and women teach us about other aspects of life as well as our faith?

• Are you afraid of aging? Why or why not?

• What has been your favorite age so far? Why?

• Peter talks about "the hidden person of the heart with the imperishable jewel of a gentle and quiet spirit, which in God's sight is very precious" (1 Peter 3:3–4). How can you cultivate this type of beauty?

chapter seven

Striking a Healthy Balance

A few years ago I was an avid runner. Sometimes I'd run with friends, but mostly I liked to run alone. This was my time to think without any distractions. I'd fall into the rhythm of running, and my thoughts somehow broke apart from one big, mixed-up jumble and became more lucid and free flowing. It was during my runs that I problem solved, set goals that had nothing to do with fitness, and prayed.

I'm not much of a runner anymore. A chronic injury has sidelined me for now. However, I still value fitness and the way it makes me feel physically and emotionally, so I walk regularly. I often pile my smallest children into the double stroller, and my older children skip along beside me. I can't zone out as I once did; little voices constantly point out things like the puffy cloud that looks like a triceratops ambling across the sky. But it's still therapeutic to be outside, moving this body that was created to move.

One summer morning I had the rare opportunity to hit the pavement for a solo walk. Without my children as my sidekicks, I could focus on the rhythm of my legs, the quickening beat of my heart, and the sweat beads forming all over my body—all evidence that I was pushing myself physically. The sun was just beginning to break through a gauzy veil of pink clouds, but it was already hot—the oppressive kind of heat that comes to a city that shares roughly the same latitude as Casablanca. But I was happy to be alone in the elements, stretching my limbs, even if I could no longer cover as much ground as I once did.

As I enjoyed my solitary walk, something urged me to pick up the pace. I broke into a run and kept on running until my hip started screaming at me to stop. My lungs were burning slightly. The sun's heat was pressing against my skin.

I was thankful for my body's response to the exercise. It reminded me of all I'm capable of and of my strength. Yet I didn't ignore my body when it said, "Enough is enough." I slowed to a walk and did not punish myself for being weak.

Someone once told me that her sister exercised for one reason and one reason only: because she knew her body was a gift from God, and she desired to show her gratitude to him by taking care of it. That's a big driving force behind why I exercise now, too. I want to show appreciation for the body God gave me. I also want to be healthy and strong, so I can be better equipped to carry out God's will for me, which includes the seemingly endless physical work of motherhood.

When I returned home and started pulling off my sneakers, I realized how far I'd come. There was a dark stretch of my life when I could admire this line of thinking while having no idea how to make it my own. At that time, I exercised not because it made me feel strong or grateful and, sadly, not because I wanted to honor God. I exercised only because I wanted to be thin.

Sometimes my motivation for exercise was even worse. Instead of caring for my body by breaking a sweat, I wanted to punish it. If I had eaten what I considered to be too much, I'd push myself harder and longer. When I worked out in the gym, I'd be that manic lady on the elliptical trainer who was surreptitiously competing with the buff guy in the spandex, trying to see which of us could pump our arms and move our legs faster. I would push myself so hard as to take the joy out of exercise and turn something good and healthy into the trappings of sin.

Temperance Is a Virtue

When it comes to the care of our bodies—whether it's in the form of fitness, food, clothing, or even applying makeup—finding balance is never easy. As I was recovering from my eating disorder, I began to voraciously read every book I could get my hands on about women and body image. While many of the books I encountered were helpful during my recovery process, I noticed a troublesome trend in some of the texts. There were people who, upon freeing themselves of a weight obsession and body-image problem, decided that their bodies were of no importance at all. What was on the inside was the only thing that mattered.

This is a touchy subject. As the mom of daughters, I consider what kind of messages I might be sending when I tell my children that something they're wearing is inappropriate or that they shouldn't eat another cookie. I can almost hear their retorts, "But I thought my looks don't matter," or, "No food is bad, remember?"

It's true: No food is bad. But if we approach food as gluttons, then we pervert it. And while the way we look is not the cornerstone of our existence, we're neglecting a fundamental truth of our faith if we say that our bodies and how we adorn them don't matter at all. Christ suffered in the flesh. God became man—the Word Incarnate. He had a body. Part of being human means having flesh. And we should care for the flesh God has given us in a loving, respectful way.

Our bodies are the only vehicles we have for living out the lives God purposes for us. He doesn't want us to feel sluggish or out of breath. We don't find freedom in giving in to temptation. He gives us the spirit of self-control. We are set free when we overcome the desires of the flesh.

Recognizing the supremacy of the spiritual doesn't mean we say, "To heck with my body. I'm a good person with a good soul. I don't have to exercise or eat well. My body doesn't really matter." Our bodies do matter. Our souls don't work out our salvation suspended in nothingness; we stumble toward heaven in our bodies. We'd best take care of them. Getting enough sleep, exercising, and fueling ourselves with healthy food are all ways to honor our bodies, which God has given us as temples of the Holy Spirit (see 1 Corinthians 6:19). However, loving self-care is not the same as the pursuit of perfection.

In our spiritual lives we are called to be the best versions of ourselves. Not all of us are cut out to be monks, yet all of us are called to work toward a rich, meaningful prayer life. The same is true in our physical life. All God asks of us is to work toward our own realistic physical ideal—not our naturally slender friend's physique or the glam queen's perfect look. Some of us may never have sleek muscles or fit society's definition of thin. We have to accept our bodies and ourselves.

How do we find this realistic ideal and strike a healthy balance? It's not easy, but thankfully we have the virtue of temperance to guide us. The *Catechism of the Catholic Church* defines temperance as "the moral virtue that moderates the attraction of pleasures and provides balance in the use of created goods. It ensures the will's mastery over instincts and keeps desires within the limits of what is honorable" (*CCC*, #1809).

The problem with applying temperance to eating is that we can take it to mean that we can't enjoy food. But God gave us a healthy desire for food. He asks only that we eat no more than our share.

Similarly, as the Author of beauty, God gifted women, to varying extents, with a desire for physical beauty. But we cannot spend every waking hour trying to figure out how to make ourselves more beautiful, nor should we wield physical attractiveness as our power.

Practicing temperance—whether in choosing the right clothing or in choosing the right amount of food to eat—means never going to extremes. We are not meant to completely abstain from food, to punish our bodies with grueling exercise, or to hide our curves with muumuus. We can eat what is good for us, and we can embrace our feminine forms without flaunting our curves or hiding them.

Temperance is a very personal virtue. It might look different for one person than it does for another. I practice temperance, for example, when I don't weigh myself frequently, since I am prone to an obsession with the number on the scale. Yet temperance for someone who is trying to shed weight in a healthy, realistic manner might mean weekly weigh-ins to keep tabs on her progress.

Likewise, we have to be careful not to condemn others who are enjoying something that we have given up. Just because we decide coffee or chocolate or wine or refined carbs are not helping us be at our best doesn't mean we should look down on a friend who still enjoys these things.

In his classic *Mere Christianity*, C.S. Lewis explained temperance as "not abstaining, but going the right length and no further."[1] Temperance means balance. It means not allowing anything—food, fashion, the pursuit of physical beauty, our work, even our children— to replace God as the center of our lives.

Just the Right Amount

God gave us food to enjoy, but eating too much (or too little) can be a sign that something is off kilter in our spiritual life. Consider

Deuteronomy 32:15: "But Jesh'urun waxed fat, and kicked; you waxed fat, you grew thick, you became sleek; then he forsook God who made him, and scoffed at the Rock of his salvation." Israel's gluttonous and unruly ways led to more rebellious behavior and an eventual abandonment of God. When we do anything in excess—eat, drink alcohol, shop—our souls are in turmoil. We've given too much power to worldly desires and fleeting feelings of satiety and happiness, instead of turning to the ultimate Peace Giver.

If you struggle with temperance in regard to food, you're not alone. Many people don't know how to eat in an intentional, balanced way. That's why there are support groups such as Overeaters Anonymous (OA) and Light Weigh. (I have listed contact information for these and other groups in the Resources section.)

Remember, your body is not a pantry. You don't need to squirrel away food to prepare for the famine. Gently remind yourself that you will eat every day of your life.

Did your parents push you to clean your plate? You may find yourself feeling guilty because you have so much and others have so little. But scraping up every last crumb of food will do nothing to save the starving children of the world.

Remember, you are stronger than a craving. You are more thoughtful than a mindless eater. You possess the spirit of self-control. Tap into it.

To cultivate temperance specifically when it comes to food, start small. Perhaps you could make a promise to leave at least a bit on your plate at every meal. Or if you always want to take seconds, start with a small serving on your plate, slowly savor the food, and then take a moment to listen to your body. If you're still hungry, give yourself the freedom to add a little more food. These two small servings should equal only one healthy-sized meal.

If you instead pile your plate with food and promise not to go back for more, you may find yourself still pining to return to the buffet. It may not even be that you want more food but that you long for the freedom to have more. Remind yourself that you will eat again tomorrow. This is not the Last Supper.

Spiritual fasting, as mentioned in chapter two, may also be a fruitful experience for you. Setting aside an entire day to fast can make you aware of what hunger really is. Normally it won't hurt you to go hungry. But if health issues, pregnancy, or nursing prevent a full fast, why not give up a certain food for a period of time?

Several years ago I was sitting down to dinner with my parents when I noticed my mom was eating her food without salting it. My mom had always been a salt lover, so I was surprised by her restraint. I asked if she'd given up salt. She admitted that she was trying not to use it and to offer the sacrifice for a personal intention. A few years later her prayer was answered, so I asked her if she was going to start salting her food again.

"Maybe here and there," she replied, "but I don't really miss it anymore."

Periodic fasting, or giving up a certain food and "offering it up," just might help you gain mastery over food. It might help you become a more temperate person while at the same time making you healthier.

As I continue to strive for a healthy balance, I try to keep my focus on healthy habits more than the number on the scale or the number of calories that pass through my lips. I focus on how I treat my body, how many fruits and vegetables I consume, and how much I exercise. Quantitative measures of health are sometimes necessary, but overall habits are far more telling and bring me more peace.

The authenticity of our love for God is tested in our love for our neighbor—and for ourselves. How can we love our neighbors if we don't love ourselves? And how much do we really love ourselves if we abuse our bodies with too much or too little food, if we never exercise, or if we let revealing clothes turn us into ornaments to be ogled? Taking care of our bodies is an expression of love for human dignity.

The barrage of sexed-up images we see every day attests to the fact that the dignity of women is under attack. But we can counter these images by the way we live. If we nurture ourselves in mind, body, and spirit, we can model what makes a woman beautiful. We can love ourselves into loving.

Soul Food

St. Frances de Sales observed, "Deer cannot run well under two circumstances: when they are either too fat, or too lean. We are greatly exposed to temptations, both when our body is too much pampered, and when it is too much weakened. One makes it insolent with ease, and the other desperate with affliction. And as we cannot bear it when it is too fat, so it cannot bear us when it is too lean."[2]

Most of us have a healthy weight that our bodies will gravitate toward when we eat the right amount and the right kinds of food and get adequate exercise. Work on identifying this healthy weight, and try to stick within a few pounds of it.

St. Anthony the Great said, "The more man uses moderation in his life, the more he is at peace, for he is not full of cares for many things."[3] Moderate living is not meant to restrict you; it's meant to free you. Remind yourself of that the next time you're tempted to do anything in excess.

Remember, too, that God's plan is to "unite all things in Christ" (Ephesians 1:10). No diet, exercise plan, act of self-restraint, or life can fail if we invite Jesus to be at its center.

The best thing we can do when we feel out of kilter—or even when things feel settled—is to have confidence in the graces we receive through prayer and the sacraments. Consider the Catholic liturgy a microcosm of life. The celebration of Mass invites the whole person—spirit, soul, and body—to be present. There's a reason we stand and kneel at certain points. Our posture during prayer can affect our openness to God.

We also receive Christ bodily. We eat him. Take the Lord's suffering and love into your body, and be transformed by it.

Exercise is a great way to give thanks for your body, but it should be more joyful than painful. St. Padre Pio said, "Our body is like a jackass that must be beaten, but just a little, otherwise it will throw us to the ground, and refuse to carry us."[4] Find a favorite exercise—whether it's dancing in your living room or taking a walk around the block—and push yourself a bit but not so much that you start to dread your workouts.

Consider the words of St. Vincent de Paul: "Let us love God, but with the strength of our arms, in the sweat of our brow."[5] We are called not only to love God with our souls and our prayerful words but with the physical exertion of our bodies, too.

St. Paul says, "Do you not know that your body is a temple of the Holy Spirit within you, which you have from God? You are not your own; you were bought with a price. So glorify God in your body" (1 Corinthians 6:19–20). What are you doing to glorify God with your body? Is your body a comfortable place for the Holy Spirit to live and work? If the answer is no, it's time to make some changes.

Keep these words of Christ close to your heart: "This is my body which is given for you" (Luke 22:19). If you abuse your body by not taking care of it or ignore the dignity of your body by punishing it for being too fat or too wrinkled, you are saying, "This is my body. I am giving it to things other than God. I defile and dishonor it."

Meditation

Imagine God appearing to you at this very moment and handing you a beautiful, tangible gift—let's say a lovely crystal vase. Would you not do everything you could to keep it clean, untarnished, and sparkling? Would you not add sprigs of greenery and blossoms to make it even more magnificent? You'd surely place it in a prominent place, and every time you saw it, you would be struck by its beauty and be reminded that it was a gift from your heavenly Father.

We should treat our bodies with the same care and admiration. They are God-given temples where the Holy Spirit dwells. They are vessels for our immortal souls. God's temple is holy. We are holy.

So for today, give your holy body the attention it deserves. Value yourself enough to make any necessary changes. Tank up on healthy food. Move your body because you can. Adorn it with handsome clothing. Don't let yourself or anyone else take it for granted or abuse it, because it's not really yours at all. It's a beautiful gift on loan from your Father.

If you love God, then love your body.

> *Dear God, my faith tells me I live with you here inside of me. I am called to be a living presence of your love and light. One day I'll see you face-to-face, but today I have to please you hidden within me. Please help me live a life of love and light, a life that gives others glimpses of you and your goodness. Cultivate the virtue of temperance in me, so that I can find balance and take care of my body without becoming entrenched in vanity. I want you to feel at home within me. Build me into a dwelling of goodness and love. Amen.*

For Your Reflection
- How would you define the virtue of temperance?
- How can you "glorify God in your body" (1 Corinthians 6:20)?
- What's your favorite form of exercise? Why?
- Write a thank-you letter to God for your body. Focus on everything you like about your physical self.
- Loving self-care is important. Set three realistic goals, such as getting more sleep or eating more vegetables, that will help you better nurture your "temple of the Holy Spirit." Write them down, and track your progress.

chapter eight

Creating a Healthy Future

Back in the sixth grade, I was swimming through a sea of peers in search of my school bus when I heard the oinking. I looked up to see two boys sticking their heads out of a bus window and pushing up their noses to make them look like pig snouts. At first I couldn't figure out why they were oinking, but then they pointed at me, laughed, and snorted again.

I quickly turned away, found my bus, and slipped into an empty seat. I tried to dam my eyes to keep from crying, but it was no use. So I stared out the window and watched the world through the blur of my silent tears.

It's taken years to silence that oinking; even reducing myself to a shadow of my former self did not quiet it. Equally persistent were the internal scripts that told me I was weak if I ate too much and worthless if I didn't live up to some unrealistic ideal. Self-editing was not enough for me; I needed professional help.

You may, too. The road to recovery looks different for each of us, but we should avoid spiritual bravado, the belief that if we pray harder or better the suffering will cease. Being a faithful Christian does not mean you're immune to health problems, and many body-image and eating problems are clinical in nature and demand medical attention.

So please know that this book is not intended to replace therapy or medical treatment. At its heart, this book is meant to help you open your life to God and remember that the Great Physician came to heal the sick. It's also meant to remind you that you are not alone in your struggles. Other people have carried and still carry very similar crosses.

I've learned that these crosses never completely go away; we just get better at managing them. There are still days when I have to blink and wake up and remember that I'm an adult now and not an awkward, insecure kid. And I'm responsible for raising children who will believe, in the depths of their souls, that they are God's valuable creations.

I have to silence that voice in my head that says, "You're not good enough." If I invite God into my life, I am and always will be good enough. Because of God's love, I was good enough when I was too thin and in control of every single bite that passed or didn't pass through my lips. I was good enough when I wasn't thin at all and was the victim of teasing. I am good enough now. So are you.

"How are you going to ensure a healthy future?" a counselor once asked me. At the time I thought the best answer was merely physical: by eating, by not making myself throw up, by consuming food rather than letting food consume me. She reminded me that these were small actions behind a much bigger action. "By loving yourself every day and in every way."

"OK," I said.

At first it all sounded rather self-indulgent. Then I began to put God into the equation. How could I truly love God if I did not love myself, one of his beloved children? My biggest enemy, my harshest critic, I realized, was myself. I did not like the person I was, and I sought affirmation in all the wrong places—the scale, thinness, the mirror—to fill the deep well of longing in my soul.

Even after I was considered physically recovered, it wasn't until I started paying more attention to my relationship with God that my real healing began. And the healing continues. Much like a recovered or dry alcoholic, I've come to see that I face an ongoing process of restoration that will, with God's grace, bring me closer and closer to his image for me.

I cannot endorse one particular form of treatment, one prayer, or one surefire way to overcome vanity, eating disorders, incessant yo-yo dieting, or food addictions. What I can say with certainty is that God is the ultimate thirst quencher. It's not until we let him in, allowing his graces and his mercy to rain down on us, that our inner wells can start to overflow. That's when we find that we have plenty of love to share.

Want to free yourself from an obsession with dieting, weight, or appearance? Start by reminding yourself every single day of God's love for you. Replace society's idea of beauty with God's. Perhaps you need to replace with God's language the hurtful words of a family member or an adolescent boy.

You are a beloved child of God. But please remember this, too: You are human. You cannot expect to eat perfectly, look perfect, or be perfect. When you stumble, pick yourself up, even if you have to do it again and again.

I used to think, when my old inner demons started creeping back into my life, that it was a sign of failure or moral weakness. But the saints have shown me that part of the human condition is to struggle with the same sins and suffering over and over again. Once I accepted the fact that I'd probably always have to be on guard against spiritual attacks related to food and my weight, I began to really recover.

Perhaps a past of binging, restricting, or purging comes back to haunt you from time to time. Maybe you have to fight hard battles against vanity, gluttony, and shame. But with God's saving power, every new day is a gift, an opportunity to detach yourself from tormenting thoughts about food or how you look and to attach yourself to God. Remember, we all hunger for God, more than we hunger for a big bowl of ice cream or a perfect physique.

When I was recovering from my eating disorder, I would wake up each morning and remind myself that I wanted God more than I wanted to be thin. Likewise, I learned to view daily exercise as a way of giving glory to God. Now I literally try to walk with the Lord. While my heart rate goes up, my prayers do, too.

Gratitude also goes a long way in helping me accept my setbacks, my failings, and even my flaws. Paul reminds us in Philippians to be grateful for what we have—not miserable about what we want or what we once had. "I have learned, in whatever state I am, to be content. I know how to be abased, and I know how to abound; in any and all circumstances, I have learned the secret of facing plenty and hunger, abundance and want. I can do all things in him who strengthens me" (Philippians 4:11–13).

We can learn to be content when we're carrying around a few extra pounds and when we're at our ideal weight, when we're hungry and when we're filled, when we're thirty and when we're fifty, when life is easy and when it is tough. We are what we are, and life is what it is, but God is bigger than any cross we bear.

This is why I try to start each day by acknowledging all that I have—a healthy family, strong legs, a warm smile, a roof over my head—and all that I do right. I suggest a maxim such as, "Lord, I am so grateful. I want all that I have."

I also work at replacing disparaging thoughts about my body and appearance with edifying ones. And if I can't rid myself completely of the mental garbage, I try to not give these negative thoughts a say in my life. Instead I allow God's medicinal words to penetrate my mind and my soul. God created me. I am his handiwork. And oh, how grateful I am that he created me and has blessed me with this beautiful life.

Recognizing the fundamental truth of our faith—that God designed us, created us, knows us, and loves us—can help us make peace with wrinkles, weight gain, stretch marks, and all the other signs of the life that is ours. God calls us to live by faith and not by sight. Let's try to see ourselves through the eyes of faith.

Why not take things a step further and see everyone through the eyes of faith? Withhold judgments based on appearance. Try not to assume things about overweight or thin people. Appreciate all body types and all ages. Recognize the beauty of God in everyone, and teach your children to do the same. "How greatly to be desired are all his works, and how sparkling they are to see!" (Sirach 42:22).

And on days when you overeat, berate your body, or agonize over the wrinkles that are signs of the life you have lived, take a deep breath and start anew. Consider going to confession for added renewal and strength. Forgive yourself, and remember that you cannot fall far enough off the path to be out of reach of God's grace.

God does not expect perfection—just continued effort. When a new day dawns, do not dredge up past mistakes. Consider the words of St. Paul, and move "forward to what lies ahead" (Philippians 3:13).

Above all, do not lose heart my friends. Every day is a battle against the world, the flesh, and the devil. This is a part of the human condition. Every day we will have to combat self-love and self-indulgence. And it's a fight worth fighting. "For whatever is born of God overcomes the world; and this is the victory that overcomes the world, our faith" (1 John 5:4).

St. Ignatius of Loyola said, "In a time of desolation, never forsake the good resolutions you made in better times. Strive to remain patient—

a virtue contrary to the troubles that harass you—and remember you will be consoled."[1]

God knocks on our hearts, but we have to open ourselves to him for his healing to take hold of our lives. And we have to believe we can be healed. We have to believe we can live without mindless munching. We have to believe we can free ourselves from an obsession with thinness and youth. We have to believe in an all-loving, all-powerful God who makes all things possible.

"Go; let it be done for you as you have believed" (Matthew 8:13). You have a choice: You can believe you're nothing and you can't be saved, or you can believe in the redeeming power of Christ and his overwhelming love for you.

To believe, we must pray. Prayer may not change circumstances; get ready for it to change you. A healthy future depends on an active prayer life. You won't really know God's love for you until you open up a dialogue and begin to have a relationship with him. Perseverance in prayer offers the most extreme makeover of all.

Put your hope in the Lord, and you'll have the endurance to make it to the finish line, where inner peace lies. You "shall run and not be weary," you "shall walk and not faint" (Isaiah 40:32). Prayer is your Gatorade. It will keep you going. It is where you meet God, where you will see that he never leaves you.

When I feel weak or frustrated, when I have a day that makes it apparent that I'm not completely over my body hang-ups, I join Paul in saying, "I can do all things in him who strengthens me" (Philippians 4:13). God is my strength.

God is your strength, your refuge. You will want nothing—not slimmer hips, ageless skin, perfect hair, or a Big Mac—if you trust in him. Believe that he loves you, all of you, including the parts you wish to hide and the parts you're eager to show the world. He is waiting to heal you, to fill your emptiness with his love and his goodness and his hope.

You were given new life in the Resurrection; embrace that new life. Our resurrected Lord says, "Peace be with you" (John 20:19). This is my prayer for you too: that you find freedom, happiness, self-acceptance, and most of all, peace in God's complete love for you.

I have chosen to close with a prayer of St. Teresa of Avila, through which I've found great solace whenever I've been faced with anxiety over my body, food, or any other aspect of my life.

> Let nothing worry you;
> Nothing dismay you;
> Everything passes;
> God does not change.
> If you have patience
> You can do anything
> Those who have God
> Want for nothing;
> God alone is enough.
>
> —St. Teresa of Avila[2]

For Your Reflection

- What is holding you back from becoming the person God wants you to be? How can you overcome these stumbling blocks?
- Write your hopes for the "new you."
- What do you struggle with the most: fear of aging, impatience with your postpartum body, obsessing over food, sloth that keeps you from exercising? What underlying emotions might feed these struggles?
- How close have you been to God in different chapters of your life? How does your relationship with the Almighty impact the way you view your body?

• Write down some key Scripture passages or quotes from the saints that are sprinkled throughout this book, and post them where you'll see them throughout your day. Allow these bites of wisdom to inspire you to build a healthier future. Here are a few I've found helpful:

The Spirit helps us in our weakness. (Romans 8:26)

It is for discipline that you have to endure.... He disciplines us for our good, that we may share his holiness. For the moment all discipline seems painful rather than pleasant; later it yields the peaceful fruit of righteousness to those who have been trained by it. (Hebrews 12:7, 10–11)

Since...Christ suffered in the flesh, arm yourselves with the same thought, for whoever has suffered in the flesh has ceased from sin, so as to live for the rest of the time in the flesh no longer by human passions but by the will of God. (1 Peter 4:1–2)

Commit your work to the LORD,
and your plans will be established. (Proverbs 16:3)

Turn away from evil.
It will be healing to your flesh
and refreshment to your bones. (Proverbs 3:7–8)

So, whether you eat or drink, or whatever you do, do all to the glory of God. (1 Corinthians 10:31)

You formed my inward parts,
you knitted me together in my mother's womb.
I praise you, for I am wondrously made. (Psalm 139:13–14)

Food is meant for the stomach and the stomach for food.... The body is not meant for immorality but for the Lord, and the Lord for the body. (1 Corinthians 6:13)

Do you not know that your body is a temple of the Holy Spirit within you, which you have from God? You are not your own; you were bought with a price. So glorify God in your body. (1 Corinthians 6:19–20)

Food will not commend us to God. We are no worse off if we do not eat, and no better off if we do. (1 Corinthians 8:8)

notes

Introduction

1. Statistics are from the National Eating Disorders Association, www.nationaleatingdisorders.org.

Chapter One: Media: The Distorted Mirror

1. John Beevers, trans., *The Autobiography of St. Thérèse of Lisieux: The Story of a Soul* (New York: Image, 2001), pp. 127–128.

2. Eileen Egan and Kathleen Egan, eds., *Blessed Are You: Mother Teresa and the Beatitudes* (New York: MJF, 1992), p. 38.

3. Beevers, p. 2.

Chapter Two: Hunger Pangs

1. John Vianney, "On Gluttony," www.saints.sqpn.com.

2. Francis de Sales, *Introduction to the Devout Life*, 40th anniversary ed. (Point Roberts, Wash.: Eremitical, 2009), pp. 147–148.

3. Margaret of Cortona, as quoted in Danielle Bean and Elizabeth Foss, *Small Steps for Catholic Moms* (North Haven, Conn.: Circle, 2010), p. 354.

4. Pope Benedict XVI, Angelus Reflection, November 6, 2005, www.vatican.va.

Chapter Three: Achieving Real Beauty

1. John Paul II, *Gratissimam Sane,* Letter to Families, no. 20, February 22, 1994, www.vatican.va.

2. John Paul II, *Mulieris Dignitatem*, Apostolic Letter on the Dignity and Vocation of Women, nos. 30, 31, August 15, 1988, www.vatican.va.

3. Joseph Ratzinger, "The Feeling of Things, the Contemplation of Beauty," Message to the Communion and Liberation Meeting, August 24–30, 2002, www.vatican.va.

4. Augustine, as quoted in Carlo Cremona, "Care for the Sick and the Fathers of the Church," www.vatican.va.

5. Rob Houston, ed., *The Human Body: An Illustrated Guide to Its Structure, Function, and Disorders* (New York: DK, 2007), p. 17.

6. Houston, p. 114.

Chapter Four: Cocreating Life

1. Jean Baptist De La Salle, as quoted in Carol Kelly-Gangi, ed., *The Essential Wisdom of the Saints* (New York: Fall River, 2008), p. 15.

2. John Paul II, Letter to Women, June 29, 1995, no. 2, www.vatican.va.

3. John Vianney, as quoted in Kelly-Gangi, p. 100.

Chapter Five: Like Mother, Like Daughter

1. John Paul II, Letter to Women, no. 12.

2. John Paul II, *Mulieris Dignitatem*, no. 10.

Chapter Six: Aging Gracefully

1. Katharine Drexel, as quoted at saints.sqpn.com.

2. Robert Ellsberg, ed., *Duty of Delight: The Diaries of Dorothy Day*, August 2, 1972 (Milwaukee: Marquette University Press, 2008), p. 510.

3. Rita of Cascia, as quoted in Ronda Chervin, *Quotable Saints* (Oak Lawn, Ill.: CMJ Marian, 2003), p. 139.

4. Elisabeth Leseur, *The Secret Diary of Elisabeth Leseur: The Woman Whose Goodness Changed Her Husband from Atheist to Priest* (Manchester, N.H.: Sophia Institute, 2002), pp. 58–59.

5. Ignatius of Loyola, as quoted in Kelly-Gangi, p. 16.

6. Anthony of Padua, quoted at www.st-anthony.medal.com.

Chapter Seven: Striking a Healthy Balance

1. C.S. Lewis, *Mere Christianity* (New York.: Touchstone, 1996), p. 76.

2. Francis de Sales, p. 148.

3. Anthony the Great, as quoted in Bean and Foss, p. 46.

4. Padre Pio, as quoted in Kelly-Gangi, p. 64.

5. Vincent de Paul, as quoted in Kelly-Gangi, p. 2.

Chapter Eight: Creating a Healthy Future

1. Ignatius of Loyola, as quoted in Kelly-Gangi, p. 36.

2. Teresa of Avila, lines written in her breviary, adapted from *Christian Prayer* (New York: Catholic Book, 1985), p. 1591.

Recommended Reading

Bowes, Peggy. *The Rosary Workout.* Waterford, Mich.: Bezalel, 2010.

Cash, Thomas. *The Body Image Workbook.* Oakland, Calif.: New Harbinger, 2008.

De Sales, Francis. *Introduction to the Devout Life.* Point Roberts, Wash.: Eremitical, 2009.

Loehr, Gina. *Choosing Beauty: A 30-Day Spiritual Makeover for Women.* Cincinnati: Servant, 2009.

Pollan, Michael. *Food Rules: An Eater's Manual.* New York: Penguin, 2009.

———. *In Defense of Food: An Eater's Manifesto.* New York: Penguin, 2009.

Shannon, Marilyn M. *Fertility, Cycles, and Nutrition: Self-care for Improved Cycles and Fertility...Naturally!* 4th ed. Cincinnati: Couple to Couple League, 2009.

Thibodeaux, Mark E. *God, I Have Issues: 50 Ways to Pray No Matter How You Feel.* Cincinnati: St. Anthony Messenger Press, 2005.

Valentine, Helen, and Alice Thompson. *Better Than Beauty: A Guide to Charm.* San Francisco: Chronicle, 2002.

Vost, Kevin. *Fit for Eternal Life.* Manchester, N.H.: Sophia Institute Press, 2007.

Websites

First Place 4 Health

FirstPlace4Health.com: A Christ-centered weight-loss and healthy-living program.

Light Weigh

LightWeigh.com: A Catholic spiritual growth and weight-loss program

National Eating Disorders Association

NationalEatingDisorders.org: An organization committed to providing help and hope to those affected by eating disorders, including sufferers and family members. Eating Disorders Hotline: 1-800-931-2237.

Overeaters Anonymous

OA.org: A program of recovery from compulsive eating using the Twelve Steps and Twelve Traditions of Alcoholics Anonymous. Worldwide meetings and other tools provide a fellowship of experience, strength, and hope, where members respect one another's anonymity. OA is not just about weight loss, gain, or maintenance. It addresses physical, emotional, and spiritual well-being.

The 3D Plan

3DYourWholeLife.com: A faith-based program for eating right, living well, and loving God.

For additional information, please visit KateWicker.com and click on the "Weightless" link.

ABOUT THE AUTHOR

Kate Wicker is a wife, mom of four, and journalist. She is a senior writer and health columnist for *Faith & Family* magazine as well as a regular contributor to Inside Catholic, Faith & Family LIVE! CatholicMom.com, and Catholic Womanhood of the Catholic News Agency. She has written for various regional and national media, including *Atlanta Parent,* Catholic Exchange, *Children's Ministry* magazine, *Pregnancy* magazine, and *Woman's Day.* Visit her website at KateWicker.com.